The Crypto Bridge

ISO 20022, XRP, and
the Next Financial Revolution

Bruce Goldwell

Copyright © 2024 by Bruce Goldwell
All rights reserved.

No part of this book may be reproduced, distributed, or transmitted in any form or by any means, including photocopying, recording, or other electronic or mechanical methods, without the prior written permission of the publisher, except in the case of brief quotations embodied in critical reviews and certain other noncommercial uses permitted by copyright law. For permission requests, write to the publisher at the address below.

Disclaimer

This book is provided for informational and educational purposes only. The author does not intend to offer financial, legal, or investment advice. All information, analysis, and opinions expressed in this book are based on the author's research and personal views as of the date of publication.

Readers are encouraged to conduct their own research and seek the guidance of a qualified financial advisor or investment professional before making any financial decisions. The author and publisher expressly disclaim any liability for any direct or indirect loss or risk incurred as a result of the information provided in this book.

This book should not be considered a recommendation to buy, sell, or hold any specific investment or asset, nor does it endorse any specific cryptocurrency or financial instrument.

Table of Contents

Dear Reader..5
Preface...6
Introduction...10
Chapter 1: 12
Chapter 2: 16
Chapter 3: 22
Chapter 4: 29
Chapter 5: 36
Chapter 6: 47
Chapter 7: 53
Chapter 8: 59
Average Daily Transactions via SWIFT.........................69
Market Cap 72
Potential Market Cap 76
Comprehensive Market Cap 81
More Financial Sectors..84
Hypothetical Market Cap..89
$1,000 XRP?..95
How to Get Started with XRP.......................................102
BONUS MATERIAL..104
About the Author...214

Dear Reader

As you explore *ISO 20022 and the Future of Finance*, you'll see how this global messaging standard is reshaping the way banks, institutions, and digital asset projects connect. ISO 20022 isn't just an upgrade—it's the foundation for a unified financial system where traditional finance and blockchain can work seamlessly together.

But here's what makes this moment even more urgent: certain cryptocurrencies—most notably **XRP**—are already positioned to thrive in this new environment. Ripple's XRP is not only ISO 20022-compliant, it's backed by **over 1,700 institutional contracts** with banks, corporations, and payment providers worldwide. Court disclosures, combined with moves from NYSE, NASDAQ, and Cboe toward *spot XRP ETFs*, signal that a massive influx of capital could soon flow into assets ready to operate in the post-ISO 20022 world.

Analysts estimate that if just 5–10% of anticipated ETF capital flows into XRP, it could mean **hundreds of billions in market demand**—and price projections in the triple or even quadruple digits. Add in lower interest rates and global adoption of real-time, compliant payment systems, and the stage is set for one of the most significant financial revaluations in history.

Because timing is critical, I'm including **BONUS access to my book *XRP: The Breakout Blueprint*** with your purchase. This exclusive section will show you how to understand the market forces at play, why the window for retail investors may be closing, and the exact steps I used to position myself for the coming shift.

As ISO 20022 adoption accelerates, the difference between those who simply understand the standard and those who act on it could be life-changing. I invite you to read every chapter with both curiosity and urgency—because the future of finance isn't coming, it's already here.

Preface

Why I Wrote *The Crypto Bridge:*

The idea for this book came to me during a visit to the emergency room at the VA Medical Center. **While speaking with several veterans,** I found myself explaining XRP, ISO 20022, and the seismic shifts about to occur in the financial markets worldwide. As much as I wanted to convey the importance of these topics, I realized I was not adequately prepared to provide clear and comprehensive verbal advice. That moment made it clear to me that writing this book would be a far more effective way to communicate this critical information. By putting these ideas into writing, I could provide veterans—and anyone interested—a resource to understand XRP, ISO 20022, and their roles in the future of finance. This book is my attempt to share what I believe is an urgent and transformative message.

Welcome to *The Crypto Bridge: ISO 20022, XRP, and the Next Financial Revolution*. This book is designed to provide you, the reader, with an in-depth exploration of a rapidly evolving landscape where traditional finance meets cutting-edge blockchain technology. Whether you are a seasoned crypto enthusiast, an investor looking for emerging opportunities, or simply someone intrigued by the future of finance, this book offers valuable insights that clarify ISO 20022's importance and the role XRP may play in the global economy.

In creating this guide, we harnessed the analytical powers of innovative AI tools, including Iask.AI and ChatGPT, to curate and synthesize the most relevant and up-to-date information available. Along with input from the author, this collaborative approach allowed us to dive deep into the complexities of cryptocurrency, compliance, and the transformative impact of ISO 20022. Our aim is to bring you clear, concise, and accurate insights that demystify how the ISO 20022 standard can bridge traditional financial systems with blockchain technology, setting the stage for a new era of interoperability and efficiency in finance.

In this book, you will discover how ISO 20022 is helping to standardize the exchange of financial information globally, creating a common language for banks, corporations, and blockchain-based assets like XRP. We'll explore the profound implications of this standard on cross-border payments, compliance, and the movement of value across financial markets. Additionally, we address one of the most pressing questions within the crypto community: What might the future value of XRP look like? By examining real-world data, projected adoption scenarios, and market insights, we'll shed light on the various factors that could influence XRP's valuation, providing you with an informed perspective to consider.

This book invites you to envision a future where digital assets like XRP operate seamlessly within the existing financial ecosystem, facilitating transactions with speed, security, and unparalleled efficiency. *The Crypto Bridge* serves as both a guide and a conversation-starter, challenging some of the common myths and misconceptions around the value and role of XRP.

Get ready to embark on a journey through one of the most exciting frontiers in finance, where tradition and innovation converge, and where the future of value exchange is being redefined. Welcome to the next financial revolution.

NOTE:
It is absolutely vital that you read this book in its entirety to fully understand the monumental changes unfolding in the world of finance. Across the globe, a seismic shift is taking place—an unprecedented transformation that will reshape economies, investment opportunities, and the very fabric of financial systems as we know them. Missing even a single chapter could mean

missing out on the opportunity of a lifetime.

Consider this: In just the last 30 days, XRP has experienced an extraordinary surge, climbing from the low $0.50s to over $2.50 per token—a monumental leap that reflects its growing adoption and the evolving landscape of global finance. However, to truly grasp the magnitude of XRP's potential, we must compare its current market cap with the scope of the global financial system.

At a market capitalization of approximately $140–150 billion, XRP is making waves. But when placed alongside the broader financial markets, it becomes evident that this is merely a drop in the ocean:

- The **global cross-border payments market** is estimated at **$2.5 quadrillion** annually.
- **SWIFT**, the dominant system for international payments, processes transactions in **$trillions** per day.
- The **global banking liquidity pool**—funds maintained by banks to ensure smooth operations—stands at over **$25 trillion**.

These numbers highlight the staggering scale of the financial markets XRP aims to revolutionize. A market cap of $140 billion barely scratches the surface of the opportunities available as blockchain technology and digital assets like XRP redefine how value is transferred worldwide.

As adoption increases and financial institutions and governments begin leveraging XRP for liquidity, efficiency, and speed, the potential for growth is unprecedented. XRP's current valuation is just the beginning of what could be one of the most transformative shifts in financial history.

Read through to the end of this book to gain the full picture of what's happening in the world of finance. By doing so, you'll be better equipped to position yourself for this once-in-a-lifetime opportunity.

As of December 8, 2024, this visual representation highlights the staggering scale of global financial markets compared to XRP's current market capitalization. The 15 blue squares, each representing $10 billion, illustrate XRP's approximate market cap of $150 billion. In comparison, the SWIFT network, depicted with red squares, dwarfs XRP, with each red square equaling the combined value of 10 blue squares. Beyond this, the global transfer market is represented by green rectangles, with each rectangle symbolizing $27 trillion. This stark contrast emphasizes that XRP's market cap is just scratching the surface of the immense financial landscape, which spans into the quadrillions annually. As XRP's adoption and utility grow, its potential to capture a significant share of these markets becomes increasingly apparent.

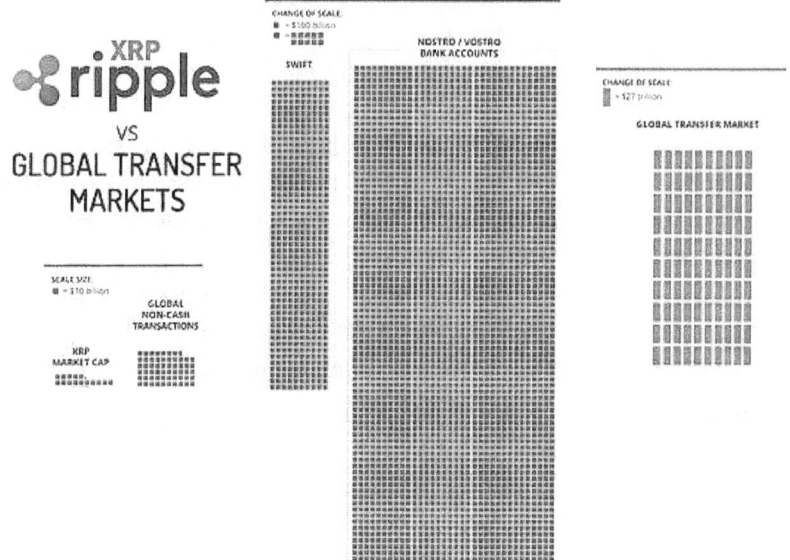

Disclosure: This image is a modified version of the original image by Kenny Nguyen @mrnguyen007 located at https://x.com/mrnguyen007/status/1863689703880331272 .

Introduction

In the constantly evolving world of finance, efficient communication across global borders has long been an elusive goal. For decades, financial institutions have operated with fragmented messaging systems, each one limited by proprietary formats, local compliance rules, and varying standards. To bridge this gap, the International Organization for Standardization (ISO) introduced ISO 20022, a messaging standard that unifies the language of electronic transactions across banks, payment networks, and even nations. Initially designed to address the complexities of traditional finance, ISO 20022 has come to represent a broader vision: creating a seamless, standardized communication pathway between all participants in the global financial ecosystem.

The power of ISO 20022 lies in its ability to convey vast amounts of structured data with unparalleled transparency and efficiency. Unlike legacy formats, this standard enables the transmission of enriched data, improving the accuracy of information, supporting compliance with regulatory requirements, and reducing the operational risks of miscommunication. The adoption of ISO 20022 holds the promise of transforming not only how transactions are executed but also how financial institutions interact on a global scale. Major entities, such as SWIFT, have already started the shift to ISO 20022, with full adoption mandated for traditional financial systems by 2025.

However, ISO 20022's influence does not stop at traditional finance. In recent years, this standard has expanded into the world of blockchain and cryptocurrency. Often seen as disruptors to established systems, cryptocurrencies are, ironically, now turning to ISO 20022 as a way to integrate with and enhance traditional financial infrastructure. By aligning with ISO 20022, compliant cryptocurrencies—such as XRP, Cardano (ADA), and Stellar (XLM)—gain access to broader financial markets, enhance their compatibility with institutional systems, and open the door to mainstream adoption. This move not only bridges a critical gap between traditional and digital finance but also highlights the growing interdependence between the two worlds.

In this book, we will delve into the profound impact of ISO 20022 on both financial institutions and the cryptocurrency industry. We will explore how ISO 20022's structured messaging benefits traditional finance, why certain cryptocurrencies are aligning with the standard, and what this means for the future of blockchain technology. By examining key ISO 20022-compliant digital assets, such as XRP, Quant (QNT), and Algorand (ALGO), readers will gain insights into how these assets are positioning themselves at the intersection of technology and finance, preparing for a new era of interoperable, efficient, and secure global transactions.

As you read on, you'll uncover the potential of ISO 20022 to change the financial world as we know it—bringing clarity to complex data exchanges, enhancing the security of transactions, and building a bridge between decentralized finance and the global banking system. By the end, you'll not only understand what ISO 20022 means but also appreciate why its adoption is one of the most pivotal moments in the history of both traditional and digital finance.

This is the story of ISO 20022—a standard that could very well become the backbone of finance in the digital age.

Chapter 1:

The Basics of ISO 20022

ISO 20022 is not just another messaging standard; it represents a foundational shift in how data is communicated across the global financial landscape. Conceived in 2004 by the International Organization for Standardization (ISO), ISO 20022 was born out of the need for a unified approach to financial messaging. Its purpose was clear: to replace the complex web of regional and proprietary standards with a single, interoperable format that could facilitate seamless, transparent, and reliable data exchange across banks, payment systems, and institutions worldwide.

1.1 Understanding ISO 20022's Purpose

At its core, ISO 20022 is about simplification and consistency. Global finance relies on the accurate and timely exchange of information across borders, institutions, and currencies. Yet, for decades, each bank or financial system had its own unique messaging formats, with each country often adding additional requirements. This fragmented system was cumbersome, prone to errors, and resource-intensive. ISO 20022 was developed to address these challenges by introducing a universal standard, one that could enable clear and structured communication between any two financial entities in the world.

The ISO 20022 standard is fundamentally different from its predecessors, like the SWIFT MT format, which relied on proprietary code systems that were difficult to adapt to the fast-paced evolution of finance. By using XML (Extensible Markup Language) and, in some cases, ASN.1 (Abstract Syntax Notation), ISO 20022 provides a language for data that is adaptable, flexible, and rich in detail. This adaptability allows ISO 20022 to be used across a variety of financial domains, including payments, securities, foreign exchange, and trade services.

1.2 The Technical Foundations of ISO 20022

ISO 20022's strength lies in its structured approach to data, which makes it both flexible and powerful. At the heart of ISO 20022 are three key components:

1. **The Dictionary**: The central dictionary is a shared repository where all data elements are defined and categorized. Each data element in the dictionary has a specific meaning, ensuring that every transaction detail—such as the sender, receiver, amount, and transaction purpose—is universally understood. This dictionary structure eliminates ambiguity, providing clarity and precision in communication.

2. **The Modelling Methodology**: ISO 20022 uses a modeling methodology to map each transaction or communication event. This allows for a standard format that accommodates complex information, such as detailed payment instructions or intricate securities settlements, within a single message. This modeling approach makes ISO 20022 scalable, ensuring that as new financial products and services emerge, the standard can be adapted without a complete overhaul.

3. **The XML/ASN.1 Protocols**: Unlike previous messaging standards, ISO 20022 utilizes XML as its core syntax, allowing messages to be both machine-readable and easily interpretable by software systems. XML's flexibility supports the structured data necessary for complex financial transactions, while its standardization across technology platforms ensures that ISO 20022 messages can be processed across different systems without loss of information. ASN.1, an alternative syntax, supports certain applications requiring compact, binary message formats.

1.3 Key Benefits of ISO 20022 in Traditional Finance

The benefits of ISO 20022 are profound and far-reaching, touching nearly every aspect of financial messaging:

- **Enhanced Data Quality**: ISO 20022 enables approximately ten times more data to be included within a single message than traditional formats. This enrichment allows for more accurate reporting, enhances compliance checks, and reduces the potential for fraud. The level of detail available through ISO 20022 also improves crime risk management, as more data can be analyzed through machine learning and AI for real-time monitoring and detection.

- **Regulatory Compliance**: In a landscape where regulatory compliance is paramount, ISO 20022 provides detailed, structured information that supports a wide range of compliance needs, from Anti-Money Laundering (AML) checks to Know Your Customer (KYC) requirements. Its standardized data format also enables financial institutions to respond more swiftly and accurately to regulatory inquiries.

- **Improved Straight-Through Processing (STP)**: One of the main operational benefits of ISO 20022 is that it enables more transactions to pass through systems without manual intervention. This "straight-through" processing (STP) minimizes errors, reduces delays, and enhances the overall customer experience by streamlining complex payment processes.

- **Cross-Border Harmonization**: ISO 20022 harmonizes global payment systems, eliminating the translation errors and delays associated with disparate messaging formats. By supporting universal, cross-border transactions, ISO 20022 enables faster, more reliable communication between financial institutions, increasing the overall efficiency of the global financial network.

- **New Revenue Streams**: By providing detailed transaction data, ISO 20022 opens opportunities for financial institutions to offer new data analysis solutions and value-added services. Enhanced liquidity management, for instance, is one area where banks can benefit from ISO

20022's data richness, allowing for more effective cash and liquidity management services.

1.4 The Timeline of ISO 20022 Adoption

The journey of ISO 20022 adoption has been gradual but steady, with various deadlines and mandates depending on regions and entities. For example:

- **SWIFT's Transition**: The SWIFT network, which facilitates most international bank-to-bank communications, has been moving toward ISO 20022 adoption, mandating full implementation for cross-border payments by 2025.

- **US Mandate**: In the United States, financial institutions are required to be ISO 20022-compliant by March 2025. As one of the largest financial markets in the world, the U.S.'s adoption will significantly impact global implementation.

- **Global Deadlines and Regional Variances**: Many countries are aligning with SWIFT's deadlines, while some have chosen to adopt the standard earlier. For example, Europe's Target2 system has already transitioned to ISO 20022, serving as an early model for other regions.

As these deadlines approach, financial institutions worldwide are accelerating their efforts to become compliant, modernize their infrastructures, and ensure their systems are ISO 20022-ready. For many, the cost of implementation and the complexity of transitioning from legacy systems pose challenges, but the long-term benefits of ISO 20022 are widely acknowledged.

Chapter 2:
ISO 20022's Role in Modernizing Financial Systems

With the adoption of ISO 20022 well underway, financial institutions are positioned to move toward a new era of communication, defined by transparency, efficiency, and interoperability. For decades, global financial systems have operated on disjointed messaging standards, leading to bottlenecks, high costs, and complex reconciliation efforts. ISO 20022 introduces a solution to these issues, promising not only to improve the structure of financial messaging but also to pave the way for real-time, cross-border transactions, integration with blockchain technology, and enhanced regulatory compliance.

In this chapter, we'll explore the transformative impact of ISO 20022 on financial systems, examine the transition from legacy formats, and discuss the importance of this standard for real-time global payment infrastructures.

2.1 The Transition from Legacy Formats to ISO 20022

Historically, financial messaging has relied on a patchwork of standards, with the SWIFT MT (Message Type) format leading the way in cross-border payments. However, as financial transactions become increasingly complex and data-driven, legacy formats are struggling to keep pace. ISO 20022 was designed to overcome these limitations by replacing proprietary, region-specific protocols with a universal standard.

Key differences between ISO 20022 and legacy formats:

- **Data Enrichment**: ISO 20022 allows for the transmission of ten times more data than the SWIFT MT format, enhancing detail in each transaction, from payer information to transaction purpose. This enriched data supports a clearer picture of each transaction, improving transparency and enabling automation.
- **XML-Based Structure**: Unlike legacy systems that

depend on fixed, proprietary codes, ISO 20022 is built on the flexible XML format, which can adapt to evolving data needs. XML's human-readable and machine-readable structure is a boon for digital transformation, facilitating smooth integration with advanced technologies.

- **Real-Time Compatibility**: The transition to ISO 20022 supports real-time processing, allowing banks and payment systems to process transactions instantly instead of in end-of-day batches. This speed is essential in a world where real-time payments are quickly becoming the norm.

With its enriched data structure, adaptable XML format, and real-time capability, ISO 20022 is positioned as a foundational standard for the future of finance.

2.2 ISO 20022 in Action: Cross-Border Payment Modernization

Cross-border transactions have traditionally been plagued by inefficiencies, as they require communication between financial institutions that often use incompatible messaging systems. ISO 20022 brings a universal language that streamlines the cross-border payment process, enabling transactions to flow seamlessly from one financial institution to another, regardless of geographic or institutional barriers.

How ISO 20022 enhances cross-border payments:

1. **Interoperability**: ISO 20022 creates a common messaging language that allows banks and financial institutions to interact more effectively, even across borders. This increased interoperability means that payment information is conveyed accurately and without the need for complex conversions.

2. **Reduced Costs and Faster Processing**: By standardizing payment messaging, ISO 20022 reduces the need for manual intervention and reconciliation. This automation lowers operational costs and accelerates transaction

speeds, which benefits consumers and businesses alike.

3. **Transparency and Traceability**: The detailed data structure of ISO 20022 enables full transparency in each transaction, allowing for end-to-end traceability. This transparency is critical for compliance, fraud prevention, and dispute resolution in cross-border payments.

2.3 Enhancing Regulatory Compliance with ISO 20022

The financial industry operates in a highly regulated environment, where institutions must meet strict Anti-Money Laundering (AML) and Know Your Customer (KYC) standards. ISO 20022 facilitates compliance by providing detailed and structured data in each transaction, which aids in identifying, monitoring, and reporting suspicious activities.

Key compliance benefits of ISO 20022:

- **Improved Reporting and Auditability**: ISO 20022's enriched data fields provide comprehensive transaction details that can be automatically aggregated for regulatory reporting, simplifying the audit process and reducing compliance costs.

- **Enhanced Fraud Detection**: The structured data available in ISO 20022 allows financial institutions to analyze transaction patterns more effectively, supporting machine learning and artificial intelligence applications in fraud detection. Institutions can identify unusual patterns and flag them for investigation in real-time.

- **Standardized KYC Data**: ISO 20022 enables the consistent collection of KYC information across financial systems, which not only reduces duplication of efforts but also enhances data accuracy. By ensuring that KYC data is standardized and easily accessible, ISO 20022 simplifies compliance checks and regulatory reporting.

2.4 ISO 20022's Role in Real-Time Payment Systems

Real-time payments (RTP) are becoming the new standard in many parts of the world, with customers expecting immediate transaction processing for both domestic and international transactions. The traditional batch-processing methods, where transactions are processed at set intervals, are increasingly inadequate for the fast-paced global economy. ISO 20022 supports the infrastructure needed to make real-time payments possible on a global scale.

Why ISO 20022 is essential for real-time payments:

- **Unified Framework**: ISO 20022's universal messaging structure makes it ideal for real-time payment systems, as it eliminates the need for system-specific adaptations or custom messaging formats.

- **Enhanced Customer Experience**: Real-time payments improve the customer experience by providing immediate confirmation of transactions. With ISO 20022, payment messages can include enriched data, providing clarity on transaction details for customers.

- **Increased Liquidity Management**: Real-time payment capabilities allow financial institutions to manage liquidity more effectively. With immediate settlement of funds, banks can reduce risk exposure and optimize cash flow.

As countries around the world develop their own real-time payment systems, ISO 20022 is becoming the standard of choice, enabling seamless integration between domestic systems and creating the potential for global, interoperable real-time payment networks.

2.5 The Global Timeline for ISO 20022 Adoption

The shift to ISO 20022 is being phased in over several years, with adoption timelines varying by country and financial institution. Major financial entities like SWIFT are leading the charge, setting key deadlines that encourage a coordinated global effort.

Key milestones in ISO 20022 adoption:

- **SWIFT's 2025 Deadline**: SWIFT, the global financial messaging network, has mandated that all cross-border payments will use ISO 20022 by November 2025. This deadline represents one of the most significant steps in standardizing global financial messaging.
- **Regional Timelines**: Some regions have already begun implementing ISO 20022. For instance, the European Central Bank's Target2 system and the Bank of England's CHAPS have adopted ISO 20022, setting an early example for other countries.
- **The United States**: In the U.S., financial institutions are required to transition to ISO 20022 by March 2025. Given the scale of the U.S. financial market, this move will significantly impact global financial messaging practices.

The staggered approach to ISO 20022 adoption allows financial institutions to prepare for the transition while setting the stage for universal adoption by 2025. As deadlines approach, institutions are under pressure to update legacy systems, train staff, and ensure compliance with the new standard.

2.6 Challenges and Costs of ISO 20022 Implementation

While the benefits of ISO 20022 are significant, the transition process is complex, and many financial institutions face challenges in adopting the standard:

- **Infrastructure Overhauls**: Legacy systems that were not designed to accommodate ISO 20022's enriched data fields require substantial upgrades. This overhaul can be costly, requiring both new software and extensive staff training.
- **Interim Solutions for Non-Compliant Partners**: In regions where adoption timelines differ, financial institutions must adopt interim solutions that allow them to communicate with partners who are not yet ISO 20022-compliant, which can add complexity to the migration

process.

- **Cost of Compliance**: Smaller financial institutions, in particular, may struggle with the financial burden of ISO 20022 implementation. These costs include not only software upgrades but also adjustments to internal processes and reporting systems to meet the standard's requirements.

Despite these challenges, the investment in ISO 20022 is seen as essential for institutions that wish to remain competitive in a rapidly evolving financial ecosystem.

Conclusion

ISO 20022 is not just a messaging standard; it is a blueprint for the future of finance. By offering a universal, detailed, and adaptable data structure, ISO 20022 enables a modernized, interoperable global financial network that bridges gaps between countries, banks, and customers. As the world moves closer to the 2025 deadline for universal adoption, ISO 20022 is expected to become the foundation for real-time payments, seamless cross-border transactions, and enhanced regulatory compliance.

In the following chapters, we will explore how this powerful standard is now influencing the world of cryptocurrency. As digital assets begin to align with ISO 20022, they stand to benefit from the same advantages that traditional financial institutions are gaining. Through ISO 20022, cryptocurrency is positioned to integrate with the mainstream financial system, further broadening its utility and adoption on a global scale.

Chapter 3:

ISO 20022 in Digital Assets – Bridging Traditional Finance and Cryptocurrency

As ISO 20022 reshapes traditional finance, its influence is also extending into the world of digital assets, specifically in how cryptocurrencies and blockchain technology interact with mainstream financial systems. By enabling standardized data exchanges between banks and compliant blockchain platforms, ISO 20022 acts as a bridge, positioning cryptocurrency to operate within the framework of traditional finance while still preserving its decentralized nature.

ISO 20022's promise of interoperability, enriched data, and regulatory alignment is particularly appealing in the context of cryptocurrency. For certain digital assets that prioritize compatibility with global financial systems, ISO 20022 compliance provides a means of both legitimizing and expanding their applications within established financial networks. This chapter explores how ISO 20022 facilitates the integration of cryptocurrencies into mainstream finance, the key players leading this adoption, and its potential impact on the DeFi sector.

3.1 Cryptocurrency and ISO 20022: Enhancing Compatibility with Financial Institutions

Cryptocurrencies, initially viewed as disruptors to traditional finance, are increasingly aligning with ISO 20022 to leverage its standardized messaging framework. The standard enables cryptocurrencies to engage in seamless data exchanges with banks and other financial institutions, providing a pathway for digital assets to be integrated into legacy financial systems.

The benefits of ISO 20022 for cryptocurrency include:

- **Seamless Integration with Banks**: ISO 20022 provides a clear structure that allows compliant cryptocurrencies to interact directly with banking systems. For example, ISO 20022-compliant digital assets such as Ripple (XRP) and

Stellar (XLM) can be used in cross-border transactions, with payment details conveyed in a format that banks understand.

- **Enhanced Transparency and Security**: The enriched data fields of ISO 20022 offer clear transaction details, which enhances security and helps reduce fraud. For cryptocurrencies, which are sometimes viewed with skepticism by financial institutions, this added transparency is valuable, building trust and improving the legitimacy of compliant assets.

- **Global Reach and Compliance**: ISO 20022 compliance signals a commitment to meet global regulatory standards, making it easier for institutions to work with cryptocurrencies that align with the framework. This opens up a broader market for compliant digital assets, allowing them to be used in international transactions.

These benefits allow ISO 20022-compliant cryptocurrencies to gain traction with financial institutions, where streamlined communication and clear data are essential. Projects such as XRP, XLM, and QNT are at the forefront of this movement, adopting ISO 20022 as a means of establishing their relevance and value within traditional finance.

3.2 ISO 20022 and Its Impact on Decentralized Finance (DeFi)

While DeFi seeks to create financial services that operate independently of traditional intermediaries, ISO 20022 could still play a role in this space. Here's how ISO 20022 impacts DeFi:

1. **Improved Interoperability with Traditional Finance**: DeFi platforms are designed to offer decentralized financial services, but ISO 20022 can enhance their ability to communicate with traditional financial systems. By aligning with ISO 20022, DeFi projects can bridge the gap between decentralized platforms and the banking sector,

making it easier for institutions to integrate with DeFi applications.

2. **Enabling Regulatory Compliance**: DeFi platforms often face challenges in meeting regulatory standards, which can hinder their appeal to institutional investors. ISO 20022's structured data model enables better tracking and reporting of transaction details, which can help DeFi projects align with compliance frameworks. This compliance capability may encourage more traditional financial institutions to participate in DeFi by enabling services that are transparent and regulatory-ready.

3. **Boosting Transparency and Security**: DeFi applications rely on smart contracts and blockchain transparency, but fraud and security risks can still pose challenges. ISO 20022 can enhance transaction transparency, allowing DeFi platforms to integrate additional layers of risk management. This added security may help reassure potential users and institutions wary of DeFi's less regulated structure.

4. **Cross-Platform and Cross-Chain Transactions**: ISO 20022 enables seamless cross-platform transactions, allowing DeFi users to move assets between different blockchain ecosystems and traditional financial institutions. For example, a DeFi platform that integrates ISO 20022-compliant cryptocurrencies like Quant (QNT) could facilitate cross-chain transactions in a manner that is fully compatible with banking systems, opening up DeFi liquidity pools to institutional investors.

5. **Expanding Institutional Adoption of DeFi**: With ISO 20022's structure supporting compliance, DeFi projects may attract institutional investors who previously hesitated due to concerns about transparency and regulatory alignment. This standardization may encourage these investors to enter the DeFi space, providing liquidity

and accelerating the growth of decentralized finance.

While ISO 20022 does not replace the decentralized ethos of DeFi, it can enhance its integration with established financial systems, which could be transformative for the sector. As DeFi platforms consider aligning with ISO 20022, the potential for wider adoption and increased regulatory acceptance grows, paving the way for DeFi to mature as a more secure, transparent financial service alternative.

3.3 Key Players in the ISO 20022-Compliant Crypto Space

Several cryptocurrencies have embraced ISO 20022 to ensure they remain compatible with traditional financial systems and accessible to institutional users. Here are some prominent ISO 20022-compliant digital assets:

- **Ripple (XRP)**: Ripple's XRP token has gained traction in cross-border payments and remittances, offering a fast, low-cost alternative to traditional banking. With ISO 20022 compliance, XRP can engage directly with financial institutions, providing a bridge between crypto and fiat currency.

- **Stellar (XLM)**: Stellar's XLM token focuses on connecting financial institutions and providing accessible financial services to underserved communities. By adopting ISO 20022, Stellar enables transparent cross-border transactions, enhancing its integration with banks and payment systems worldwide.

- **Quant (QNT)**: Known for its focus on blockchain interoperability, Quant leverages the Overledger protocol to connect multiple blockchain networks. ISO 20022 compliance enables Quant to facilitate cross-chain transactions and connect with traditional financial networks, supporting DeFi applications that span various blockchain ecosystems.

- **Algorand (ALGO)**: Algorand, a scalable and secure

blockchain platform, supports decentralized applications (dApps) and financial services. With ISO 20022 compatibility, Algorand is positioned to attract institutional interest by bridging DeFi and traditional finance in a way that adheres to regulatory and messaging standards.

- As of now, there are eight prominent cryptocurrencies aligned with the ISO 20022 standard, which positions them for integration with traditional financial systems. These compliant digital assets include **XRP (XRP)**, known for its efficiency in cross-border payments; **Cardano (ADA)**, a scalable and secure blockchain; **Quant (QNT)**, which focuses on interoperability across blockchains; **Algorand (ALGO)**, designed for both financial and non-financial applications; **Stellar (XLM)**, ideal for fast, low-cost transactions; **Hedera Hashgraph (HBAR)**, a high-performance ledger for enterprise applications; **IOTA (MIOTA)**, geared toward the Internet of Things (IoT) ecosystem; and **XDC Network (XDC)**, an enterprise-grade platform focusing on trade and supply chain finance. Each of these projects leverages the structured messaging capabilities of ISO 20022 to enable seamless communication and interoperability with existing financial systems, paving the way for blockchain adoption across various industries.

These ISO 20022-compliant cryptocurrencies are setting a precedent, proving that blockchain can co-exist with traditional finance. Their commitment to interoperability and regulatory compliance opens the door for broader adoption, particularly among institutional investors seeking reliable access to digital assets.

3.4 ISO 20022's Role in the Future of Digital Assets

As ISO 20022 becomes the universal messaging standard, its impact on the digital asset space will likely deepen. The standard's ability to support high data volumes and compliance makes it a natural fit for the evolving demands of both traditional finance and cryptocurrency.

Future implications include:

- **Enhanced DeFi Ecosystems**: ISO 20022 could help DeFi platforms evolve by providing more compliant, interoperable transaction models, encouraging institutional involvement and increased liquidity.
- **Unified Financial Systems**: With ISO 20022, digital assets and traditional finance are becoming more connected, creating a unified system where transactions flow seamlessly between fiat and crypto.
- **Global Regulatory Alignment**: As ISO 20022-compliant assets proliferate, cryptocurrency may achieve greater global regulatory alignment, paving the way for broader acceptance and trust from traditional institutions.

ISO 20022 is shaping a future where cryptocurrencies can operate alongside banks and financial systems with greater ease. As both sectors evolve, this standard will likely continue to foster the connection between digital assets and traditional finance, setting the stage for new financial products and services that blend the strengths of both worlds.

ISO 20022 is catalyzing change in the cryptocurrency and DeFi sectors, offering a pathway for digital assets to integrate with established financial systems while retaining the unique benefits of blockchain technology. By enabling greater interoperability, transparency, and regulatory alignment, ISO 20022 is transforming digital finance, bridging the gap between traditional finance and the rapidly evolving world of cryptocurrency.

In the following chapter, we will take a closer look at some of the specific benefits and challenges of adopting ISO 20022 for blockchain projects, examining how compliance with this standard influences everything from transaction security to global adoption potential.

Chapter 4:

Benefits and Challenges of ISO 20022 for Blockchain Projects

As blockchain technology gains ground in finance, projects that adopt ISO 20022 are positioned to reap significant benefits by aligning with global financial standards. However, the journey to compliance is not without its challenges. Adopting ISO 20022 requires navigating technical, regulatory, and operational hurdles that may prove complex for blockchain initiatives originally designed to operate outside traditional financial systems. In this chapter, we'll explore the opportunities and potential challenges that ISO 20022 compliance brings to blockchain and cryptocurrency projects.

4.1 Key Benefits of ISO 20022 for Blockchain Projects

Adopting ISO 20022 offers substantial advantages for blockchain projects, from increasing regulatory compliance to expanding market reach. These benefits make ISO 20022-compliant projects attractive to financial institutions and potential investors, both of whom value transparency, security, and interoperability.

1. Enhanced Transaction Security and Data Transparency

ISO 20022 is designed to support detailed, structured data within each message, allowing for improved tracking and transparency in financial transactions. For blockchain projects, this structure enables:

- **Increased Transparency**: The data-enriched messages within ISO 20022 allow transactions to be more detailed, reducing the risk of fraud and improving overall security. With clearer and more comprehensive transaction information, blockchain projects can offer improved traceability, providing financial institutions with greater confidence in using these assets.
- **Enhanced Security Protocols**: The enriched data structure supports advanced security measures, including

fraud detection and real-time monitoring. By incorporating ISO 20022, blockchain projects can use this additional data to deploy artificial intelligence (AI) and machine learning (ML) algorithms for proactive fraud prevention.

2. Improved Regulatory Compliance

ISO 20022's detailed data framework enables blockchain projects to meet a range of regulatory requirements, from Anti-Money Laundering (AML) standards to Know Your Customer (KYC) protocols. Compliance is critical for attracting institutional investors who need assurance that digital assets operate within regulated frameworks.

- **AML and KYC Alignment**: By supporting structured KYC data, ISO 20022-compliant blockchain projects can align with AML and KYC standards, which are essential for regulatory compliance. This alignment enhances trust and encourages financial institutions to adopt these digital assets, knowing they adhere to established compliance norms.

- **Streamlined Reporting and Auditing**: With ISO 20022, blockchain projects can report transaction data in a format that is easily interpretable by regulatory bodies, simplifying compliance audits and improving transparency. Projects that adopt the standard are better equipped to respond to regulatory inquiries, a feature that is especially valuable in jurisdictions with strict reporting requirements.

3. Expanded Global Market Reach

ISO 20022 compliance opens doors for blockchain projects to operate within the global financial ecosystem, allowing for seamless interaction with traditional financial institutions. This expanded interoperability helps blockchain projects to:

- **Gain Access to Institutional Markets**: Institutions are more likely to invest in and transact with ISO 20022-

compliant blockchain projects, as the standard's data structure and reporting capabilities meet their operational and compliance requirements. This can increase the potential market for compliant digital assets, bringing in institutional liquidity and bolstering adoption.

- **Facilitate Cross-Border Payments**: ISO 20022's interoperability allows blockchain projects to support cross-border transactions more efficiently, reaching users and financial partners in different regions without the limitations of legacy messaging formats.

4. Increased Adoption Potential for Decentralized Finance (DeFi)

As discussed in the previous chapter, ISO 20022 can benefit DeFi projects by enhancing their transparency, regulatory alignment, and interoperability with traditional finance. This alignment could encourage institutional players to engage with DeFi platforms, providing the liquidity needed for DeFi to mature and expand.

- **Institutional DeFi Participation**: ISO 20022 enables DeFi platforms to create compliance-ready solutions, appealing to institutional investors interested in the security and transparency offered by ISO 20022-aligned projects. This potential for institutional engagement makes ISO 20022-compliant DeFi projects an attractive option for those looking to bridge traditional finance and decentralized applications.

4.2 Challenges of Adopting ISO 20022 for Blockchain Projects

Despite the benefits, ISO 20022 adoption is not without its challenges. Blockchain projects face several obstacles in achieving compliance, from technical integration requirements to regulatory complexities and infrastructure costs.

1. Technical Integration with Legacy Systems

Blockchain projects that were not initially designed for ISO 20022 compliance may face technical hurdles in integrating with the standard. This challenge is especially relevant for established projects with legacy infrastructure that would need to be overhauled to accommodate ISO 20022's data structure.

- **Infrastructure Upgrades**: Many blockchain projects rely on legacy systems that may not be compatible with ISO 20022's XML-based format. Significant updates to protocols and messaging frameworks are required to enable compliance, which can be costly and resource-intensive.
- **Interim Solutions for Non-Compliant Partners**: Since not all financial institutions are ISO 20022-compliant, blockchain projects may need to implement interim solutions to interact with non-compliant entities, adding layers of complexity to operations.

2. Cost of Compliance

Achieving ISO 20022 compliance often entails significant costs, especially for blockchain projects operating on limited budgets. From upgrading infrastructure to hiring compliance experts, these costs can be a barrier for smaller projects looking to enter mainstream finance.

- **Initial Compliance Costs**: Transitioning to ISO 20022 can require substantial upfront investment, including technology upgrades, process redesigns, and staff training to meet the new data and reporting standards.
- **Ongoing Operational Costs**: Beyond initial costs, maintaining ISO 20022 compliance involves ongoing expenses related to monitoring, auditing, and regulatory reporting. For projects without institutional backing, these costs can hinder their ability to achieve compliance.

3. Regulatory Complexities Across Jurisdictions

While ISO 20022 helps streamline compliance, the regulatory landscape for blockchain and cryptocurrency is still highly fragmented. Different regions have varying requirements for digital assets, and ISO 20022 adoption does not automatically equate to regulatory approval across all jurisdictions.

- **Regional Variances in Compliance Standards**: Blockchain projects aiming for global reach must navigate compliance with different regional standards, which may have additional requirements beyond ISO 20022. For example, the European Union's regulations may differ from those in the United States, requiring nuanced compliance strategies.

- **Evolving Regulatory Expectations**: As governments continue to refine their stance on blockchain technology, regulatory expectations may shift, potentially requiring projects to update their ISO 20022 implementation to meet new standards. This evolving landscape demands that blockchain projects remain agile and responsive to changing regulations.

4. Balancing Decentralization with Compliance

For blockchain projects focused on decentralization, achieving ISO 20022 compliance can present a philosophical and operational challenge. While ISO 20022 can enhance interoperability and compliance, it may also require projects to make concessions in terms of privacy, governance, or operational control.

- **Privacy Concerns**: The detailed data required by ISO 20022 can conflict with the privacy-focused nature of certain blockchain projects. Projects that prioritize user privacy may find it challenging to incorporate the standard without compromising on their core principles.

- **Governance Adjustments**: ISO 20022 compliance may require some blockchain projects to adjust their governance models, particularly those with decentralized structures. Ensuring alignment with ISO 20022 could necessitate changes in governance, such as increased regulatory oversight, which may not align with the goals of certain decentralized platforms.

4.3 Case Studies: Success Stories and Lessons Learned

To illustrate the practical application of ISO 20022, let's explore case studies of blockchain projects that have successfully adopted the standard, highlighting their benefits and the challenges they encountered:

1. **Ripple (XRP)**: Ripple is an early adopter of ISO 20022, using it to enhance cross-border payment efficiency. With partnerships with major financial institutions, Ripple's compliance with ISO 20022 has enabled XRP to operate within traditional financial networks, paving the way for a future where digital assets and fiat currencies are seamlessly integrated.

2. **Stellar (XLM)**: Stellar adopted ISO 20022 to expand its reach in underserved financial markets. With ISO 20022 compliance, Stellar has been able to create a bridge between financial institutions and unbanked populations, using the standard to enable low-cost, cross-border transactions with greater transparency and traceability.

3. **Quant (QNT)**: As a platform focusing on blockchain interoperability, Quant adopted ISO 20022 to connect various blockchain networks with traditional finance. Through the Overledger protocol, Quant has demonstrated how ISO 20022 can be used to support cross-chain transactions, creating a model for DeFi projects looking to facilitate seamless interoperability.

Each case study underscores the value of ISO 20022 compliance in broadening market reach, enhancing regulatory alignment, and building trust with financial institutions. However, these success stories also illustrate the resource investment and strategic planning needed to implement ISO 20022 effectively.

For blockchain projects, ISO 20022 represents both an opportunity and a challenge. While the standard enables enhanced security, regulatory alignment, and access to global markets, achieving compliance requires significant investments in infrastructure, compliance expertise, and governance adaptations. For projects that are able to overcome these challenges, ISO 20022 offers a pathway to greater adoption and legitimacy, positioning them to thrive in a financial landscape that increasingly values interoperability and transparency.

In the next chapter, we will delve deeper into specific ISO 20022-compliant cryptocurrencies, analyzing their features, use cases, and impact on both traditional finance and DeFi. By examining how these projects are leading the way in ISO 20022 adoption, we can better understand the potential of compliant digital assets in transforming the future of finance.

Chapter 5:

Leading ISO 20022-Compliant Cryptocurrencies

As traditional finance continues its migration toward ISO 20022, several cryptocurrency projects have positioned themselves at the forefront of this integration, using the standard to foster interoperability and enhance their appeal to institutional investors. ISO 20022 compliance offers these digital assets a means of bridging decentralized finance with mainstream financial systems, thereby expanding their functionality, market reach, and legitimacy.

In this chapter, we'll take an in-depth look at some of the prominent ISO 20022-compliant cryptocurrencies, exploring how each project aligns with the standard, their core use cases, and the potential impact on both traditional and decentralized finance.

5.1 Ripple (XRP): The Cross-Border Payment Pioneer

Ripple's XRP token is a well-established cryptocurrency, widely recognized for its efficiency in cross-border payments and remittances. Developed to facilitate fast, low-cost transactions, XRP has garnered significant attention from banks and financial institutions looking to streamline international transactions.

How Ripple aligns with ISO 20022:

- **Interoperability with Financial Institutions**: Ripple's ISO 20022 compliance allows its payment solutions to integrate with existing banking infrastructure. By adopting the standard, Ripple has positioned XRP to communicate seamlessly with traditional financial systems, reducing the friction of cross-border transactions.

- **Liquidity and Efficiency**: XRP acts as a bridge currency, enabling liquidity between various fiat currencies. With ISO 20022's structured messaging, Ripple can process these exchanges with enhanced transparency, speed, and security, which is particularly valuable for financial institutions dealing with multiple currencies.

Notable Partnerships: Ripple's partnerships with institutions such as Santander Bank, American Express, and Bank of America underscore its commitment to working within established financial frameworks, making XRP one of the most institutionally integrated digital assets.

Core Features:

- 1,500 transactions per second
- Cost and energy-efficient XRP Ledger Consensus Protocol
- Partnerships with major financial institutions

XRP Adoption for Cross-Border Exchange

XRP, the digital asset created by Ripple Labs, has been positioned as a solution for cross-border payments. Its adoption has been a topic of interest among various financial institutions, banks, and countries looking to enhance their payment systems. Below is a detailed examination of the entities that have agreed to use XRP or are involved in its ecosystem for cross-border exchanges.

1. Financial Institutions and Banks

Several financial institutions have partnered with Ripple to utilize XRP for cross-border transactions:

- **Santander**: The Spanish bank has integrated Ripple's technology into its payment services, allowing customers to send money internationally using XRP through its One Pay FX service.
- **American Express**: In collaboration with Ripple, American Express has explored the use of XRP for facilitating cross-border payments between the U.S. and the UK.
- **Standard Chartered**: This major international bank has also engaged with Ripple's technology to improve its cross-border payment capabilities.

- **PNC Bank**: PNC Bank has utilized RippleNet, which includes the option to use XRP for certain transactions.
- **MoneyGram**: Although not a traditional bank, MoneyGram has partnered with Ripple to leverage XRP for liquidity in cross-border transactions.

These partnerships indicate a growing acceptance of XRP as a viable option for enhancing transaction speed and reducing costs associated with international money transfers.

2. Countries Involved

While no country has officially adopted XRP as a national currency or standard method of exchange, several countries are exploring or have implemented blockchain technology that may include assets like XRP:

- **Japan**: Japan is one of the leading countries in cryptocurrency adoption and regulation. Several Japanese banks are part of the Ripple network and utilize its technology for efficient remittance services.
- **United Arab Emirates (UAE)**: The UAE has shown interest in blockchain technologies, including partnerships with Ripple to facilitate faster remittances within the region.
- **Philippines**: The Philippines is another country where Ripple's technology is being used by local banks and remittance companies to streamline cross-border payments.

3. Regulatory Environment

The regulatory landscape surrounding cryptocurrencies like XRP is crucial in determining their adoption. As of October 2023, regulatory clarity around cryptocurrencies varies significantly by jurisdiction:

- In some regions like Europe and Asia, there are more

favorable regulations that encourage banks and financial institutions to adopt blockchain technologies.
- Conversely, in jurisdictions where regulations are stringent or unclear regarding cryptocurrencies, adoption may be limited.

Overall, while many institutions have expressed interest in utilizing XRP for cross-border exchanges through partnerships with Ripple Labs, widespread adoption remains contingent on regulatory developments and technological advancements.

In summary, various banks such as Santander and American Express have integrated or tested XRP within their systems for international transactions. Countries like Japan and the UAE are also exploring these technologies but have not fully adopted them at a national level.

Overview of BRICS and XRP

The BRICS nations, comprising Brazil, Russia, India, China, and South Africa, are exploring various strategies to enhance their financial systems and reduce dependence on the U.S. dollar. One of the discussions surrounding this exploration involves the potential use of XRP, a cryptocurrency developed by Ripple Labs, for cross-border payments among these countries.

Potential Benefits of Using XRP

XRP is designed to facilitate fast and low-cost cross-border transactions. Its transaction speed is significantly faster than traditional banking systems, which can take days to process international payments. The low fees associated with XRP also make it an attractive option for BRICS countries looking to streamline their payment processes. Additionally, adopting XRP could enhance financial inclusion within these nations by providing easier access to banking services for unbanked populations.

Challenges of Adoption

Despite its advantages, the adoption of XRP by BRICS faces several challenges:

1. **Regulatory Uncertainty**: Each BRICS nation has different regulatory stances on cryptocurrencies. This lack of harmonization could hinder the widespread adoption of XRP across the bloc.
2. **Centralization Concerns**: Although Ripple claims that the XRP Ledger is decentralized, there are concerns regarding Ripple Labs' control over a significant portion of the total XRP supply. This centralization contradicts the goals of BRICS nations seeking financial independence from U.S.-based entities.
3. **Technological Integration**: Integrating XRP into existing financial systems would require substantial investment in technology and infrastructure upgrades within each country.

Current Developments

Recent reports indicate that while there is interest in utilizing XRP for cross-border payments among BRICS nations, it remains speculative at this stage. The bloc's overarching goal is de-dollarization and creating a multipolar financial system that allows greater autonomy from Western influence. Given this context, some analysts suggest that it may be more feasible for BRICS to develop their own digital currencies or payment systems rather than relying on a cryptocurrency closely tied to a U.S.-based company like Ripple.

Additionally, there are rumors about BRICS potentially introducing a gold-backed currency as a more stable alternative to the U.S. dollar, which aligns better with their objectives.

In summary, while there is potential for BRICS countries to explore using XRP in their payment systems due to its efficiency and cost-effectiveness, significant hurdles such as regulatory uncertainty and centralization concerns make widespread adoption unlikely at this time. Instead, developing independent digital currencies or alternative payment solutions seems more aligned with their goals.

5.2 Stellar (XLM): Empowering Financial Inclusion

Stellar's XLM token aims to address issues of financial inclusion by enabling fast, low-cost cross-border payments. With a focus on connecting financial institutions and providing financial services to underserved populations, Stellar has embraced ISO 20022 to enhance its interoperability and appeal to financial entities around the world.

How Stellar aligns with ISO 20022:

- **ISO 20022 Messaging for Financial Institutions**: By adopting ISO 20022, Stellar allows financial institutions to use its platform for cross-border payments in a way that aligns with global standards. This compatibility increases Stellar's accessibility for traditional financial institutions, furthering its mission of financial inclusion.

- **Low-Cost Transactions**: Stellar's consensus mechanism enables low-cost transactions, making it ideal for smaller remittances that benefit from ISO 20022's data-rich, structured format. This structure aids in tracking and provides transparency, appealing to financial entities focused on accessible financial services.

Key Collaborations: Stellar's partnerships with IBM and MoneyGram highlight its commitment to financial inclusion. These collaborations leverage ISO 20022 to create accessible, cross-border payment solutions.

Core Features:

- Fast and low-cost transactions
- Stellar Consensus Protocol (SCP) for scalability and

security
- Partnerships with IBM and MoneyGram for accessible cross-border payments

5.3 Quant (QNT): The Interoperability Protocol

Quant focuses on blockchain interoperability, allowing multiple blockchains to communicate through its Overledger protocol. With ISO 20022 compliance, Quant has extended its interoperability beyond blockchain networks, enabling communication with traditional financial systems and broadening its applications.

How Quant aligns with ISO 20022:

- **Cross-Platform Transactions**: Quant's Overledger protocol is designed to facilitate communication between different blockchains. ISO 20022 compatibility enhances Quant's ability to interact with financial institutions, making it easier to bridge decentralized platforms with centralized financial systems.
- **DeFi and TradFi Integration**: By adopting ISO 20022, Quant enables DeFi applications that are interoperable with traditional finance, potentially supporting use cases such as lending, payments, and cross-chain asset transfers in a compliant, regulated manner.

Use Case Potential: Quant's ISO 20022 integration positions it as a valuable tool for DeFi platforms seeking to expand their reach to institutional investors and mainstream financial systems.

Core Features:

- Blockchain interoperability protocol (Overledger)
- Capable of handling high transaction volumes without performance loss
- Decentralized governance model with an engaged developer community

5.4 Algorand (ALGO): Sustainable and Scalable Blockchain Solutions

Algorand is a blockchain platform known for its scalability, low transaction costs, and environmentally friendly proof-of-stake (PoS) consensus mechanism. By adopting ISO 20022, Algorand enhances its compatibility with financial institutions, making it an attractive option for enterprise-level applications.

How Algorand aligns with ISO 20022:

- **ISO 20022 for Secure, Scalable Transactions**: Algorand's ISO 20022 compliance supports secure, fast, and scalable transactions that are compatible with traditional financial systems. This structure is particularly valuable for institutions looking for blockchain solutions that are both environmentally friendly and operationally efficient.
- **dApp Development and Smart Contracts**: With ISO 20022, Algorand is suited to support decentralized applications (dApps) that require transparent, cross-border data exchanges. By enabling structured messaging, Algorand can create scalable financial solutions with enriched data capabilities.

Institutional Appeal: Algorand's sustainable design and ISO 20022 compliance make it attractive to institutional investors, particularly those looking for eco-friendly blockchain solutions.

Core Features:

- Low-cost transactions and PoS consensus mechanism
- Support for smart contracts and dApps
- High scalability with low environmental impact

5.5 Hedera HashGraph (HBAR): Enterprise-Grade Blockchain Solutions

Hedera Hashgraph is a public ledger that aims to provide fast, secure, and fair decentralized applications (dApps) for enterprise solutions. Using a unique consensus algorithm, Hedera enables high throughput and low-cost transactions, making it ideal for applications that require fast, secure data exchanges.

How Hedera aligns with ISO 20022:

- **ISO 20022 and Enterprise Integration**: With ISO 20022, Hedera can offer enterprise solutions that communicate directly with traditional financial systems. The standard enables Hedera to support applications that require both high throughput and regulatory compliance.

- **Security and Compliance**: Hedera's compliance with ISO 20022 helps ensure that its enterprise applications adhere to regulatory requirements, building trust among institutions seeking secure and compliant blockchain solutions.

Use Cases for Enterprise-Level DeFi: Hedera's ISO 20022 alignment positions it as a solution for enterprise-level DeFi applications, potentially enabling secure, transparent asset transfers and data exchanges between financial systems.

Core Features:

- Unique Hashgraph consensus algorithm for high efficiency
- Support for smart contracts and decentralized applications (dApps)
- Energy-efficient and suitable for high-volume applications

5.6 XDC Network (XDC): Blockchain for Trade Finance

XDC Network is a hybrid blockchain platform tailored to global trade and supply chain finance. With ISO 20022 compliance, XDC Network aims to facilitate secure and efficient cross-border transactions, enhancing transparency in trade finance.

How XDC Network aligns with ISO 20022:

- **Hybrid Blockchain Design**: XDC Network's hybrid structure combines the benefits of public and private blockchains, allowing for secure data exchanges that align with ISO 20022's regulatory standards.
- **Supply Chain Applications**: By leveraging ISO 20022, XDC Network provides transparency in supply chain finance, enabling secure tracking of goods, materials, and payments. This is particularly valuable for institutions focused on managing complex, cross-border supply chains.

Core Features:

- Hybrid blockchain supporting both public and private transactions
- High transaction speed (up to 2,000 transactions per second)
- Designed to meet regulatory requirements for supply chain tracking

5.7 IOTA (MIOTA): Enabling the Internet of Things (IoT)

IOTA is a unique distributed ledger tailored for the Internet of Things (IoT) ecosystem, utilizing the Tangle (a Directed Acyclic Graph, or DAG) instead of a traditional blockchain. ISO 20022 compliance enables IOTA to provide structured, transparent data exchanges in IoT applications, facilitating interoperability with financial and non-financial systems.

How IOTA aligns with ISO 20022:

- **Data-Driven Applications**: ISO 20022's structured messaging allows IOTA to facilitate feeless microtransactions and secure data transfers within the IoT, where devices need to exchange data efficiently and securely.
- **Quantum-Resistant Security**: IOTA's Tangle structure is

designed to be quantum-resistant, which makes it a unique solution for high-security data exchanges within the IoT and beyond. ISO 20022 compliance further enhances the security and transparency of these exchanges.

Core Features:

- Feeless transactions tailored for IoT
- Quantum-resistant and data-oriented design
- High scalability for handling large data volumes

The leading ISO 20022-compliant cryptocurrencies showcase the transformative potential of aligning digital assets with traditional financial standards. By adopting ISO 20022, these projects enhance their appeal to financial institutions, enabling secure, transparent, and compliant cross-border transactions. As traditional and decentralized finance converge, ISO 20022-compliant cryptocurrencies are set to play a crucial role in shaping the future of a unified, interoperable financial ecosystem.

In the next chapter, we will explore the future of ISO 20022 in both traditional finance and the cryptocurrency sector, looking at how the standard is likely to evolve as financial systems become increasingly interconnected.

Chapter 6:
The Future of ISO 20022 in Finance and Cryptocurrency

ISO 20022 is already a game-changer in traditional finance, providing a framework for more efficient, transparent, and data-rich communication across global payment systems. However, its full impact is still unfolding, particularly as digital assets and blockchain technology continue to integrate with traditional finance. As ISO 20022 adoption progresses, the future holds exciting possibilities for unified financial systems, streamlined compliance, and greater cross-industry interoperability.

This chapter explores the potential future developments for ISO 20022, its role in the next generation of financial technology, and its implications for cryptocurrency and decentralized finance.

6.1 ISO 20022 as the Foundation for a Unified Financial Ecosystem

As ISO 20022 becomes the global standard for financial messaging, it is set to act as a bridge between traditional and digital finance. The standard's adaptability and enriched data structure make it an ideal foundation for a financial ecosystem where both fiat currencies and cryptocurrencies coexist seamlessly.

The path toward a unified ecosystem includes:

- **Increased Interoperability**: ISO 20022's universal messaging framework will enable traditional banks, blockchain projects, and DeFi platforms to communicate effortlessly. This interoperability will support seamless cross-border transactions, integrating digital assets into global financial markets without the need for intermediary conversion processes.

- **A Bridge for Fiat and Digital Currencies**: As central banks worldwide explore the development of Central Bank Digital Currencies (CBDCs), ISO 20022's structured data format will likely serve as a foundation for these digital fiat currencies to interact with cryptocurrencies. By providing a common language, ISO 20022 facilitates cross-currency interoperability, allowing CBDCs and cryptocurrencies to coexist in the financial ecosystem.

- **Enhancing Global Trade Finance**: ISO 20022's potential extends into industries beyond banking, particularly in sectors like supply chain finance and global trade. Blockchain projects like XDC Network are already exploring ISO 20022's applications in trade finance. As more projects adopt the standard, ISO 20022 could become a universal data format across industries, reducing bottlenecks in cross-border trade and supporting efficient supply chain management.

6.2 ISO 20022 and Decentralized Finance (DeFi): A Catalyst for Institutional Adoption

As DeFi matures, ISO 20022 could become a crucial factor in its broader acceptance by financial institutions and regulators. By providing a data-rich messaging structure that aligns with compliance requirements, ISO 20022 opens up opportunities for DeFi projects to engage with traditional finance on a much larger scale.

Future implications of ISO 20022 for DeFi:

- **Increased Institutional Participation**: ISO 20022-compliant DeFi platforms could become attractive to institutional investors seeking exposure to decentralized assets. With data structure that supports compliance with Anti-Money Laundering (AML) and Know Your Customer (KYC) requirements, DeFi platforms aligned with ISO 20022 can offer institutions the transparency and security they need.

- **Enhanced DeFi Product Offerings**: ISO 20022 could support DeFi applications designed for complex financial products like bonds, derivatives, and asset-backed securities, which require extensive data. By utilizing ISO 20022, DeFi platforms can handle these products with the same level of detail and regulatory oversight as traditional financial institutions, creating a bridge for institutional-grade DeFi products.

- **Potential Regulatory Acceptance**: As ISO 20022 continues to support regulatory compliance, DeFi projects that adopt this standard may encounter fewer regulatory hurdles. This alignment with traditional finance standards could make it easier for DeFi platforms to obtain approval and operate in regulated markets, further increasing adoption potential.

6.3 Advancements in Security, Compliance, and Data Transparency

ISO 20022 offers enhanced security and transparency through structured data, a feature that could play a significant role in the future of blockchain, DeFi, and financial regulation.

Security and Transparency Enhancements:

- **Improved Fraud Detection**: With ISO 20022's detailed data structure, financial institutions and DeFi platforms can monitor transaction patterns more closely, enabling real-time fraud detection. Machine learning and AI can further enhance this capability, using ISO 20022 data to identify suspicious activity and improve security across the financial ecosystem.

- **Data-Driven Compliance**: ISO 20022 supports data-rich transactions that simplify regulatory reporting and audits, which are increasingly data-dependent. As compliance standards evolve, ISO 20022 will allow financial institutions and blockchain projects to meet reporting requirements more easily, potentially reducing compliance costs and increasing accuracy in regulatory filings.

- **Transparency for Users and Regulators**: The structured data fields within ISO 20022 provide clarity in transaction details, which benefits users and regulatory authorities. Enhanced transparency makes it easier for consumers to understand transaction fees, purposes, and counterparties, while also enabling regulators to conduct audits more efficiently.

6.4 The Quantum Financial System and ISO 20022

The Quantum Financial System (QFS) is an emerging concept that leverages quantum computing, blockchain, artificial intelligence, and decentralized networks to create a more efficient, secure financial system. ISO 20022's universal language for financial transactions positions it as a foundational standard for QFS, as it can facilitate seamless, real-time data exchanges across advanced digital networks.

Potential impacts of ISO 20022 on QFS:

- **Unified Data Standards for Advanced Financial Systems**: ISO 20022 could become the primary messaging standard for QFS, providing the consistent data structure needed to support quantum computing applications. As financial systems transition toward quantum-ready infrastructure, ISO 20022's compatibility with advanced data handling will support QFS's adoption.

- **Real-Time Data and AI Integration**: QFS aims to process financial transactions at quantum speeds, which requires data structures that can handle real-time processing with precision. ISO 20022's data enrichment supports AI algorithms, which will be integral to QFS in managing complex transaction data, identifying risks, and making autonomous financial decisions.

- **Decentralized, Intermediary-Free Transactions**: QFS is envisioned as a system where transactions can occur without intermediaries, facilitated by blockchain and AI.

ISO 20022's standard messaging format can enhance these transactions by providing structured, compliant data that ensures consistency and transparency across decentralized networks.

6.5 Anticipating the Evolution of ISO 20022 in Cryptocurrency and Finance

As ISO 20022 continues to gain traction, its adoption will likely influence how the cryptocurrency sector and traditional finance evolve. Future iterations of ISO 20022 are expected to accommodate emerging technologies, regulatory changes, and new financial products, potentially leading to:

- **Support for Multi-Asset and Hybrid Financial Products**: As financial markets evolve, ISO 20022 may expand to accommodate hybrid products that combine fiat currencies, digital assets, and tokenized securities. These products require extensive data to account for pricing, ownership, and regulatory requirements, making ISO 20022 an ideal standard to support them.

- **Adaptability for New Financial Ecosystems**: The adaptability of ISO 20022 ensures it will remain relevant as financial technology evolves. As blockchain and DeFi platforms mature, ISO 20022 could be updated to include specific fields and protocols that accommodate smart contracts, decentralized lending, and staking, further supporting DeFi integration into mainstream finance.

- **Regulatory-Driven Iterations**: ISO 20022's evolution may be shaped by regulatory requirements, particularly as governments implement new standards for digital assets and cross-border transactions. Future versions of ISO 20022 could address specific compliance needs, making it easier for digital assets to gain regulatory approval.

The future of ISO 20022 holds vast potential for both traditional finance and the cryptocurrency space. By creating a universal messaging standard, ISO 20022 enables seamless interaction between banks, blockchain networks, DeFi platforms, and potentially even quantum financial systems. This level of integration supports the vision of a unified, interoperable financial ecosystem, one that prioritizes transparency, security, and regulatory compliance.

As ISO 20022 continues to evolve, it will likely play a central role in the modernization of finance, transforming how digital assets and traditional institutions communicate, transact, and build trust. For blockchain projects and DeFi platforms, aligning with ISO 20022 opens up a world of possibilities, making it easier for them to engage with institutional investors and thrive within a global financial network that values interoperability and innovation.

In the next chapter, we'll take a deeper dive into how ISO 20022 compliance affects investment strategies and the future of asset tokenization, examining why ISO 20022-compliant assets might be particularly attractive to investors and financial institutions alike.

Chapter 7:

ISO 20022 Compliance and Investment Strategies in Digital Assets

As ISO 20022 gains widespread adoption, digital assets that comply with the standard are well-positioned to capture the attention of investors and institutions. With the promise of interoperability, regulatory alignment, and enhanced data transparency, ISO 20022-compliant digital assets offer unique advantages that make them attractive investment options. In this chapter, we'll explore the impact of ISO 20022 on investment strategies, including its influence on portfolio diversification, institutional adoption, and the future of asset tokenization.

7.1 Why ISO 20022 Compliance is Attractive to Investors

The advantages of ISO 20022 compliance extend beyond operational efficiency and regulatory compliance. For investors, assets that align with ISO 20022 offer added transparency, security, and compatibility with traditional financial infrastructure, which are critical considerations in an increasingly interconnected financial landscape.

Key reasons ISO 20022-compliant assets appeal to investors:

1. **Regulatory Assurance and Risk Mitigation**: ISO 20022 compliance provides a structured data format that aligns with regulatory standards, enhancing transparency and reducing the risk of non-compliance. Investors value this regulatory assurance as it lowers investment risks associated with digital assets, particularly in jurisdictions with strict regulatory requirements.

2. **Improved Transparency and Data Richness**: ISO 20022's enriched data fields offer a clearer view of transaction details, providing investors with greater visibility into asset movements and ownership structures. This transparency not only builds trust but also simplifies due diligence processes, making compliant digital assets

easier to assess and track.

3. **Institutional Compatibility**: By adopting ISO 20022, digital assets can interact seamlessly with financial institutions. This compatibility is particularly important for institutional investors, who are more likely to invest in assets that integrate easily with their existing infrastructure and comply with global standards.

4. **Future-Proof Investment**: As ISO 20022 becomes the universal messaging standard, compliant assets are well-positioned to remain relevant in a future where financial ecosystems demand interoperability. For investors, this future-proofing is attractive, as it aligns with long-term investment goals.

7.2 Impact on Institutional Investment Strategies

ISO 20022 compliance opens doors for institutional investors to include digital assets in their portfolios, offering new ways to diversify and mitigate risk. Institutional investors are particularly sensitive to compliance and regulatory risks, and ISO 20022-compliant assets provide the alignment necessary for inclusion in regulated portfolios.

How ISO 20022 affects institutional investment strategies:

- **Increased Allocation to Digital Assets**: The added security, transparency, and regulatory alignment of ISO 20022-compliant digital assets may encourage institutions to allocate a larger portion of their portfolios to digital assets. This shift could lead to significant inflows of capital, especially as institutions seek to diversify and capture the potential returns offered by cryptocurrencies and blockchain-based assets.

- **Enhancing Portfolio Diversification**: ISO 20022-compliant digital assets, such as XRP, XLM, and ALGO, offer new opportunities for portfolio diversification. By combining these assets with traditional investments, institutional investors can create a balanced portfolio that leverages the growth potential of digital assets while maintaining regulatory oversight.

- **Enabling Compliance with Fiduciary Duties**: Institutional investors are bound by fiduciary duties to act in the best interest of their clients, which includes adherence to regulatory standards. ISO 20022-compliant assets provide a framework that aligns with these duties, allowing institutions to meet their compliance obligations while benefiting from digital asset exposure.

7.3 ISO 20022 and the Rise of Asset Tokenization

Asset tokenization—the process of representing real-world assets as digital tokens on a blockchain—is revolutionizing investment. ISO 20022 compliance enhances the appeal of tokenized assets by providing a standardized messaging framework that supports transparency, regulatory alignment, and global interoperability.

Benefits of ISO 20022 for asset tokenization:

- **Fractional Ownership and Increased Liquidity**: ISO 20022-compliant tokenized assets enable fractional ownership, allowing investors to buy smaller portions of high-value assets, such as real estate or commodities. This fractionalization increases liquidity and democratizes access to assets that were previously restricted to high-net-worth individuals and institutions.

- **Streamlined Cross-Border Transactions**: Tokenized assets that comply with ISO 20022 can be traded internationally with fewer barriers, as the standard's structured data aligns with regulatory requirements in multiple jurisdictions. This feature is particularly valuable for real estate and commodities markets, where cross-border investment is common.

- **Efficient Asset Management and Reporting**: With ISO 20022's enriched data structure, asset managers can track tokenized assets more effectively, making reporting and compliance simpler. For investors, this increased transparency translates to greater trust in the asset's value and security, which can lead to higher investment inflows.

Use Cases in Tokenization:

1. **Real Estate**: ISO 20022-compliant tokenized real estate allows investors to own a portion of high-value properties, with compliance standards that appeal to institutions seeking regulated real estate exposure.

2. **Commodities**: Precious metals, oil, and other commodities are increasingly tokenized, enabling investors to gain exposure without holding physical assets. ISO 20022 compliance makes it easier to trade tokenized commodities across borders and within regulated markets.

3. **Art and Collectibles**: Tokenized art and collectibles have emerged as alternative investments, and ISO 20022 compliance enhances the legitimacy and trackability of these assets, making them appealing to investors.

7.4 ISO 20022's Role in Shaping the Future of Digital Asset Investment

As ISO 20022 adoption grows, its influence on digital asset investment will continue to expand. ISO 20022-compliant assets are likely to play a central role in the next phase of financial evolution, where traditional investment vehicles, tokenized assets, and cryptocurrencies coexist in a unified financial ecosystem.

Future trends in ISO 20022-driven digital asset investment:

- **Integration with Wealth Management Platforms**: ISO 20022 compliance enables digital assets to be integrated into mainstream wealth management platforms, where they can be managed alongside stocks, bonds, and other assets. This integration could attract wealth managers to digital assets, further driving adoption among high-net-worth investors.

- **Enhanced Tokenized Exchange-Traded Products (ETPs)**: ISO 20022's structure allows for compliant tokenized ETPs, where fractional ownership of a basket of assets can be traded like traditional ETFs. These ETPs would be attractive to retail and institutional investors alike, offering exposure to digital assets with regulatory transparency.
- **Automated Portfolio Rebalancing**: ISO 20022-compliant assets allow for detailed data collection, supporting automation in portfolio management. This feature can be leveraged by robo-advisors and asset managers to create automated rebalancing strategies that align with clients' risk tolerance and compliance requirements.

7.5 Case Studies: Success Stories in ISO 20022-Compliant Digital Assets

To illustrate the impact of ISO 20022 on investment, let's examine case studies of digital assets that have successfully integrated with traditional finance, gaining traction with institutional investors:

1. **XRP and Institutional Remittances**: XRP's ISO 20022 compliance has facilitated its adoption in cross-border remittances, with major financial institutions leveraging XRP for efficient, low-cost transactions. As a compliant digital asset, XRP has gained institutional trust, leading to higher liquidity and investment inflows.

2. **Stellar (XLM) in Financial Inclusion**: Stellar's partnerships with MoneyGram and other financial service providers have enhanced its role in financial inclusion. By adopting ISO 20022, Stellar has made it possible for institutions to participate in low-cost, cross-border payments, benefiting underserved populations while attracting socially responsible investors.

3. **Algorand's Sustainable Blockchain for Enterprises**: Algorand's ISO 20022 compliance has strengthened its appeal as an eco-friendly and scalable blockchain for enterprise solutions. With a focus on sustainable finance, Algorand has garnered attention from institutions looking for environmentally responsible investments that align with regulatory standards.

These examples highlight the success of ISO 20022-compliant assets in meeting the needs of institutional investors, enhancing their credibility and fostering trust in digital asset investment.

ISO 20022 compliance is reshaping the investment landscape for digital assets, providing a foundation for transparent, regulated, and interoperable financial products. By aligning with this standard, digital assets gain credibility and accessibility, attracting institutional investors and mainstream wealth management platforms. ISO 20022's influence extends to asset tokenization, where it enables innovative investment vehicles such as tokenized real estate, commodities, and collectibles.

As digital asset investment strategies evolve, ISO 20022-compliant assets are likely to become a core component of diversified portfolios, bridging traditional finance with the digital economy. The future of digital asset investment promises to be dynamic and transformative, driven by the alignment of blockchain technology with standards like ISO 20022.

In the final chapter, we will summarize the key takeaways of ISO 20022's role in finance and cryptocurrency, and consider the long-term implications for a financial ecosystem where digital assets and traditional finance are increasingly interconnected.

Chapter 8:

Conclusion – The Future of ISO 20022 in a Connected Financial World

ISO 20022 has redefined what's possible in financial messaging by introducing a universal, data-rich framework that enhances communication between financial institutions worldwide. While initially developed to streamline traditional finance, the adoption of ISO 20022 has proven to be transformative for the cryptocurrency and blockchain space, enabling these digital assets to integrate with mainstream financial systems in ways previously thought impossible.

In this final chapter, we'll reflect on the main insights covered in this book and look toward the future, where ISO 20022-compliant assets may become integral components of a seamlessly connected, interoperable financial ecosystem.

8.1 Key Takeaways from ISO 20022's Role in Finance and Cryptocurrency

Throughout this book, we have explored the significant advantages and challenges that ISO 20022 presents to traditional finance, blockchain projects, and decentralized finance. Here are the primary insights we've uncovered:

- **Universal Financial Messaging**: ISO 20022 replaces fragmented legacy formats with a single, standardized messaging language. By enabling a common structure for data-rich transactions, ISO 20022 improves transparency, enhances data accuracy, and supports real-time processing, making financial systems more efficient and reliable.

- **A Bridge Between Traditional Finance and Cryptocurrency**: ISO 20022's adoption by digital assets like XRP, XLM, and QNT provides a bridge between fiat and crypto. This interoperability is essential for global finance, enabling digital assets to interact with banks, payment processors, and other financial entities without additional complexity.

- **Increased Appeal for Institutional Investors**: By aligning with ISO 20022, digital assets gain legitimacy in the eyes of institutional investors, who seek regulated, transparent, and compliant investment options. ISO 20022 compliance simplifies due diligence, streamlines reporting, and reduces regulatory risk, making compliant assets more attractive to institutions.

- **Enhanced Data Security and Compliance**: ISO 20022's enriched data structure facilitates secure transactions, fraud detection, and regulatory compliance. For DeFi and tokenized assets, this level of transparency is critical for meeting compliance requirements and attracting more participants to the decentralized financial ecosystem.

8.2 The Vision for a Unified Financial System

As ISO 20022 adoption progresses, it is likely to become the backbone of a globally connected financial system. The integration of ISO 20022-compliant assets into traditional finance is only the beginning of a broader shift toward a unified financial network that allows both fiat and digital currencies to coexist seamlessly.

Characteristics of a unified financial system include:

- **Cross-Border and Cross-Asset Interoperability**: ISO 20022 paves the way for financial systems where assets, whether fiat, cryptocurrency, or tokenized, can move across borders with minimal friction. This global interoperability could reduce transaction costs, shorten settlement times, and make financial services more accessible to a diverse range of users.

- **DeFi and TradFi Convergence**: As DeFi platforms embrace ISO 20022, they gain greater alignment with traditional finance, facilitating institutional adoption. This convergence is expected to reshape finance by allowing

DeFi applications to operate alongside regulated financial services, offering compliant, secure, and efficient financial solutions.

- **Support for Advanced Financial Systems**: ISO 20022's flexible framework positions it as a potential standard for quantum finance and other advanced systems. With the standard's ability to handle high data volumes and provide detailed transaction information, it supports future technologies that demand precise and scalable messaging.

8.3 Challenges and Opportunities on the Horizon

While ISO 20022's benefits are substantial, there are still challenges and opportunities that the financial sector must navigate as adoption increases. Key considerations for the future include:

- **Adapting to New Compliance Requirements**: As regulatory standards evolve, ISO 20022 will need to remain adaptable. Future updates to the standard could reflect changes in data security, AML, and KYC requirements, ensuring that ISO 20022 remains relevant in an increasingly regulated environment.

- **Scaling for Mass Adoption in Blockchain**: For blockchain and DeFi projects, scaling to meet ISO 20022 standards may require significant upgrades. However, projects that succeed in implementing the standard will likely benefit from increased credibility and market reach, positioning themselves at the forefront of digital finance.

- **Innovating with Tokenization and Digital Assets**: ISO 20022-compliant tokenization platforms can lead the way in creating new types of digital assets, such as tokenized real estate, commodities, and collectibles. As the tokenization industry matures, ISO 20022 could support the seamless trading and settlement of tokenized assets, making them more accessible to global markets.

8.4 Long-Term Implications for Investors and Institutions

ISO 20022's impact on investors and institutions is likely to expand in the coming years as more digital assets align with the standard. For financial institutions, ISO 20022 offers new ways to incorporate digital assets into their services, and for investors, it introduces compliant, data-driven investment opportunities.

Implications for the investment landscape include:

- **Broadening Access to Digital Asset Markets**: ISO 20022-compliant digital assets are expected to become more accessible across traditional investment platforms, increasing the visibility and acceptance of digital assets among mainstream investors.

- **Institutional Adoption and Asset Allocation**: ISO 20022 compliance could lead to a shift in institutional asset allocation strategies, with more funds dedicated to compliant digital assets and tokenized products. As digital assets become more regulated, their inclusion in institutional portfolios is likely to increase.

- **Driving Innovation in Asset Management**: Asset managers can leverage ISO 20022 data to develop new financial products, such as tokenized ETFs and automated portfolio strategies, enabling diversified investment options that combine traditional and digital assets.

8.5 Final Thoughts: The Future of Finance with ISO 20022

ISO 20022 stands as a cornerstone of the future financial system. Its integration into cryptocurrency and blockchain projects represents a step toward a world where financial transactions are fast, transparent, secure, and interconnected. The standard's impact on compliance, security, and interoperability is paving the way for a financial ecosystem where traditional finance and digital assets are no longer separate but mutually reinforcing.

As we move forward, ISO 20022 is set to influence a wide range of financial innovations, from quantum finance and decentralized finance to asset tokenization and real-time payment systems. This standard not only enhances the value and utility of compliant digital assets but also serves as a framework for building a global financial network that meets the needs of an increasingly digital, data-driven world.

The future of finance is bright with ISO 20022 at its foundation, supporting a new generation of financial products and services that are accessible, efficient, and globally compatible. For those who invest in and build on this standard, ISO 20022 offers an opportunity to be part of a transformative journey toward a truly interconnected financial world.

Closing Remarks

As we conclude, it's clear that ISO 20022 is more than just a messaging standard. It's a bridge to a new financial era, one where digital assets and traditional finance can coexist, offering unparalleled transparency, regulatory compliance, and global reach. Whether you are an investor, a financial institution, or a blockchain developer, understanding and engaging with ISO 20022 is essential for thriving in the future financial landscape.

Thank you for joining this exploration of ISO 20022 and its impact on the future of finance. As we continue to witness the rapid evolution of this standard, the opportunities for innovation, collaboration, and growth are boundless.

Additional Resources for Readers

To provide readers with practical insights and enhance their understanding, here are several supplemental sections designed to clarify key terminology, guide investment decisions, address common questions, and highlight the potential evolution of ISO 20022.

Glossary of ISO 20022 and Crypto-Finance Terms

ISO 20022 and blockchain each bring unique terminology that can sometimes be technical and complex. This glossary clarifies essential terms to help readers navigate the content:

- **XML (Extensible Markup Language)**: A versatile data format used in ISO 20022 to structure data for both machine and human readability, supporting consistent, data-rich communication.

- **ASN.1 (Abstract Syntax Notation)**: A data representation format sometimes used in ISO 20022 for compact, binary messaging in certain high-volume applications.

- **Overledger**: A blockchain interoperability protocol developed by Quant, allowing different blockchain networks to communicate. Essential for integrating ISO 20022 with multiple blockchain platforms.

- **Tangle**: A unique data structure used by IOTA, which differs from a traditional blockchain. Tangle is a Directed Acyclic Graph (DAG) that allows for feeless, secure transactions, particularly in IoT applications.

- **AML (Anti-Money Laundering)** and **KYC (Know Your Customer)**: Regulatory requirements that prevent illicit activities, such as money laundering and fraud. ISO 20022 enhances compliance with AML and KYC through structured data.

Checklist for Investors Assessing ISO 20022-Compliant Assets

Investors interested in ISO 20022-compliant assets can use this checklist to evaluate potential investments effectively:

1. **Compliance and Transparency**: Verify that the project aligns fully with ISO 20022, as compliant assets typically meet high standards of regulatory transparency and structured data handling.

2. **Institutional Adoption**: Assess partnerships and integrations with financial institutions or enterprise clients. Collaborations with recognized banks or companies often indicate robust and reliable technology.

3. **Project Fundamentals**:

   - **Use Case**: Determine the asset's primary purpose and real-world applicability.

   - **Scalability**: Assess whether the project can handle high transaction volumes, particularly if it aims for cross-border payments.

   - **Transaction Speed**: Look at the project's ability to process transactions quickly, as speed is essential for adoption in real-time payments.

   - **Security Protocols**: Ensure the project employs advanced security measures, including fraud detection and encryption, to safeguard transactions.

Frequently Asked Questions (FAQs)

This FAQ section answers common questions from investors, institutions, and blockchain developers, providing clarity on ISO 20022 compliance and its applications:

- **How long does it take for a blockchain project to achieve ISO 20022 compliance?** Compliance timelines can vary depending on the project's existing infrastructure, resources, and scale of operations. On average, achieving full ISO 20022 alignment can take several months, with significant time spent on infrastructure upgrades and testing.

- **What are the long-term benefits of ISO 20022 for non-financial sectors, such as supply chain management or IoT?** In sectors like supply chain management and IoT, ISO 20022 enhances data consistency and communication across networks. Its adoption can improve data tracking, transparency, and efficiency, making it ideal for any sector that relies on structured, high-volume data exchanges.

- **How can DeFi platforms benefit from ISO 20022 if they prioritize decentralization?** ISO 20022 compliance supports DeFi platforms by enabling regulatory alignment, enhancing transparency, and attracting institutional users. While decentralization remains a priority, the adoption of structured data and compliance capabilities can make DeFi platforms more appealing to investors.

Case Studies on Cross-Sector ISO 20022 Applications

These case studies illustrate how ISO 20022 can be used beyond traditional finance, showcasing its versatility and wide-ranging benefits:

- **Non-Financial Applications**:
    - **IoT with IOTA**: IOTA uses ISO 20022 to facilitate feeless transactions within the Internet of Things, providing structured messaging for data exchange between IoT devices.
    - **Global Trade with XDC Network**: In trade finance, XDC Network uses ISO 20022 to track goods and facilitate secure, compliant transactions across borders, reducing costs and improving transparency in supply chains.
- **Real-Time Payments in Practice**:

- **SWIFT and Target2**: ISO 20022's application in real-time payment systems like SWIFT and Target2 in Europe demonstrates the standard's effectiveness in enabling seamless, cross-border transactions. This implementation underscores ISO 20022's ability to streamline payment processing and reduce delays.

Timeline of Global ISO 20022 Adoption Milestones

To help readers track key ISO 20022 adoption milestones, here's a timeline summarizing regional and institutional deadlines for full implementation:

- **2023-2025**: Major banks and financial systems worldwide transition to ISO 20022, with Europe's Target2 and the Bank of England leading early adoption.
- **March 2025**: The United States mandates ISO 20022 compliance for financial institutions, setting a new standard for data consistency.
- **November 2025**: SWIFT retires its MT messaging format in favor of ISO 20022 for cross-border payments, marking a significant milestone in global finance.

This timeline provides a quick reference for readers to understand when specific regions and institutions are expected to complete their ISO 20022 transitions.

A Final Note on Emerging Trends

As ISO 20022 adoption continues, here are some emerging trends that may shape the future of finance and digital assets:

- **Potential Evolution Toward ISO 20022 v2**: If the financial world universally adopts ISO 20022, the standard may eventually evolve to support even more data fields, possibly including fields for digital identity verification and enhanced blockchain integration. An updated version could enable even richer data transfers and support additional compliance standards as technology advances.

- **Quantum-Ready Standards**: As the Quantum Financial System becomes more feasible, ISO 20022 may need to incorporate quantum-compatible cryptography, enabling secure, quantum-resistant transactions. This evolution would make ISO 20022 adaptable for the next generation of secure, high-speed financial transactions, keeping it relevant as financial technology becomes increasingly advanced.

Final Thoughts

These additional resources offer readers practical tools for navigating ISO 20022, assessing investments, and staying informed about future developments in finance and cryptocurrency. Together, they enhance the reader's understanding, ensuring they have a comprehensive toolkit for engaging with ISO 20022-compliant digital assets in the evolving global financial landscape.

Average Daily Transactions via SWIFT

The Society for Worldwide Interbank Financial Telecommunication (SWIFT) is a crucial component of the global financial infrastructure, facilitating secure and efficient communication between financial institutions. As of November 2022, SWIFT recorded an average of **44.8 million messages** sent daily through its network. These messages primarily consist of payment instructions and other financial transaction communications.

To understand the scale of transactions processed via SWIFT, it is important to note that while SWIFT itself does not transfer funds, it plays a vital role in relaying payment orders between banks. The actual value of transactions can vary significantly depending on the nature and volume of the payments being processed at any given time.

In terms of monetary value, SWIFT supports an estimated **$21 trillion** in financial payments every day. This figure encompasses various types of transactions including international wire transfers, securities settlements, and foreign exchange operations among others.

The combination of these statistics illustrates the immense scale at which SWIFT operates within the global economy, highlighting its importance as a facilitator for international trade and finance.

In summary:

- Average daily messages: **44.8 million**
- Estimated daily transaction value: **$21 trillion**

Daily Transactions in International Trade Excluding SWIFT

To determine the volume of transactions conducted on a daily basis in international trade, excluding those that go through the Society for Worldwide Interbank Financial Telecommunication (SWIFT), we need to consider several factors and data sources.

1. Understanding International Trade Volume

International trade encompasses the exchange of goods and services across borders. According to the World Trade Organization (WTO), global merchandise trade was valued at approximately $22 trillion in 2021. This figure includes both exports and imports of goods.

2. Daily Trade Calculation

To find a daily transaction volume, we can divide the annual trade value by the number of days in a year:

$$\text{Daily Trade Volume} = \frac{\text{Annual Trade Value}}{\text{Number of Days}}$$

Using the 2021 figure:

$$\text{Daily Trade Volume} = \frac{22 \text{ trillion USD}}{365} \approx 60.27 \text{ billion USD}$$

This calculation gives us an approximate daily volume for total international merchandise trade.

3. Excluding SWIFT Transactions

SWIFT primarily facilitates financial transactions between banks, which include payments related to international trade but does not encompass all forms of payment methods used in international trade. Other methods include letters of credit, documentary collections, and direct bank transfers that may not utilize SWIFT messaging.

While exact figures for transactions outside SWIFT are challenging to ascertain due to the variety of payment methods employed globally, it is reasonable to estimate that a significant portion of international trade transactions occurs without using SWIFT.

4. Estimating Non-SWIFT Transaction Volume

Research indicates that around 80% of global trade finance is conducted through traditional banking channels, which may or may not involve SWIFT directly. Therefore, if we assume that about 20% of transactions are processed via alternative methods not involving SWIFT, we can calculate:

Non-SWIFT Daily Trade Volume=Daily Trade Volume×(1−0.20)

Calculating this gives us:

Non-SWIFT Daily Trade Volume=60.27billion USD×0.80≈48.22billion USD

5. Conclusion

Thus, based on these calculations and assumptions regarding transaction methods in international trade excluding those processed through SWIFT, we arrive at an estimated daily transaction volume.

Answer: Approximately $48.22 billion USD per day in international trade transactions not including what goes through SWIFT.

Market Cap

The market cap for XRP, as well as for other cryptocurrencies, is calculated in a straightforward manner using the following formula:

Market Cap=Circulating Supply×Current Price per Token

Here's a breakdown of each component:

1. **Circulating Supply**: This is the number of tokens or coins currently available on the market and in the hands of the public. It excludes tokens held in escrow or unreleased by the project founders (e.g., Ripple's held and locked XRP).

2. **Current Price per Token**: This is the latest price at which the cryptocurrency is trading on exchanges. Market cap fluctuates as the price changes.

For **XRP**, the calculation would look like this:

Market Cap of XRP=Current Circulating Supply of XRP×Current Price of XRP

Example Calculation:

Suppose XRP has a circulating supply of **53 billion** and is trading at **$0.50** per XRP:

Market Cap=53,000,000,000×0.50=26,500,000,000USD

So, the market cap of XRP would be **$26.5 billion** in this example.

Important Notes for Other Cryptocurrencies:

- **Fully Diluted Market Cap**: Some projects also report the "fully diluted market cap," which is the market cap if all tokens in the total supply (not just circulating supply) were released at the current price.

- **Price Volatility**: The market cap fluctuates with the price, which is highly volatile in crypto markets.

Hypothetical Market Cap Projections for XRP in Global Financial Transactions

If XRP were to capture a portion of the daily transactions that go through SWIFT and the remaining international trade, its valuation could see substantial growth. Here's a breakdown of the current transaction volume and how it translates into XRP's hypothetical market cap at various levels of adoption.

Current Global Financial Transaction Volumes

1. **SWIFT Daily Transactions**: $21 trillion per day
2. **Non-SWIFT International Trade Transactions**: Approximately $48.22 billion per day

This brings the **total daily transaction volume** (SWIFT + Non-SWIFT) to approximately:

$$21 \text{ trillion} + 48.22 \text{ billion} = 21.048 \text{ trillion USD per day}$$

Assumptions for XRP Market Cap Calculations

- **Circulating Supply**: We will use an approximate circulating supply of 53 billion XRP.
- **Value Transfer Rate**: For simplicity, we assume each XRP token could hypothetically process the equivalent daily transaction volume it captures from the global financial sector.

Market Cap Calculation Scenarios

1. Scenario 1: XRP Captures 25% of Daily Global Transaction Volume

If XRP captures 25% of the total daily transaction volume:

$$0.25 \times 21.048 \text{ trillion USD} = 5.262 \text{ trillion USD}$$

Assuming each XRP in circulation represents a share of this 25% market capture, the **price per XRP** would be calculated by dividing the total captured value by the circulating supply.

Price per XRP=

53billion XRP / 5.262trillion USD

= 99.28USD per XRP

Therefore, the **market cap at 25% capture** would be:

5.262trillion USD

2. Scenario 2: XRP Captures 35% of Daily Global Transaction Volume

If XRP captures 35% of the total daily transaction volume:

0.35×21.048trillion USD=7.367trillion USD

Price per XRP at this capture rate:

Price per XRP=

53billion XRP / 7.367trillion USD

=139.00USD per XRP

The **market cap at 35% capture** would be:

7.367trillion USD

3. Scenario 3: XRP Captures 50% of Daily Global Transaction Volume

If XRP captures 50% of the total daily transaction volume:

0.50×21.048trillion USD=10.524trillion USD

Price per XRP at this capture rate:

Price per XRP=

53billion XRP / 10.524trillion USD

=198.56USD per XRP

The **market cap at 50% capture** would be:

10.524trillion USD

Summary of Hypothetical Market Cap Projections for XRP

Capture Rate	Daily Transaction Volume Captured (USD)	Hypothetical Price per XRP (USD)	Hypothetical Market Cap (USD)
25%	5.262 trillion	99.28	5.262 trillion
35%	7.367 trillion	139.00	7.367 trillion
50%	10.524 trillion	198.56	10.524 trillion

Conclusion

If XRP were to capture a portion of the global financial transaction volume, even at a fraction of SWIFT and non-SWIFT transactions, the potential for a high market cap becomes evident. At a 25% capture rate, XRP would reach a market cap of **$5.26 trillion**, whereas a 50% capture could theoretically see its market cap rise to **$10.52 trillion**. This hypothetical scenario illustrates the potential of XRP as a bridge currency, facilitating global transactions on a massive scale if adopted widely by financial institutions.

Potential Market Cap

for XRP in Global Financial Markets

To envision XRP's potential market cap, let's examine scenarios where XRP captures 10% and 50% of the daily transaction values in key global financial markets, such as Forex, stock, commodity, derivatives, and bond markets. Given the immense daily transaction volumes in these markets, even a small fraction of adoption could translate into significant value for XRP.

1. Foreign Exchange Market (Forex)

The Forex market is the largest and most liquid in the world, with a daily trading volume estimated at around 6.6 trillion USD.

- **If XRP captures 10% of the Forex market**:
    - The transaction value captured would be approximately 660 billion USD.
    - Dividing 660 billion USD by XRP's circulating supply of 53 billion tokens would yield an estimated price of around 12.45 USD per XRP.
    - The market cap would be about 660 billion USD.
- **If XRP captures 50% of the Forex market**:
    - The transaction value captured would be approximately 3.3 trillion USD.
    - Dividing 3.3 trillion USD by 53 billion XRP would yield an estimated price of around 62.26 USD per XRP.
    - The market cap would be approximately 3.3 trillion USD.

2. International Stock Markets

International stock markets have a combined daily trading volume in the hundreds of billions, with an estimated market cap of around 100 trillion USD globally.

- **If XRP captures 10% of the global stock market's daily trading volume**:
    - Assuming a daily trading volume of 500 billion USD, 10% of this would be approximately 50 billion USD.
    - Dividing 50 billion USD by 53 billion XRP would give an estimated price of around 0.94 USD per XRP.
    - The market cap would be around 50 billion USD.
- **If XRP captures 50% of the global stock market's daily trading volume**:
    - 50% of 500 billion USD would amount to approximately 250 billion USD.
    - Dividing 250 billion USD by 53 billion XRP would yield an estimated price of 4.72 USD per XRP.
    - The market cap would be around 250 billion USD.

3. Commodity Markets

The daily trading volume in international commodity markets, including the CME and ICE, is estimated at around 100 billion USD.

- **If XRP captures 10% of the commodity market**:
    - 10% of 100 billion USD is approximately 10 billion USD.
    - Dividing 10 billion USD by 53 billion XRP would result in an estimated price of 0.19 USD per XRP.
    - The market cap would be around 10 billion USD.
- **If XRP captures 50% of the commodity market**:

- 50% of 100 billion USD would be around 50 billion USD.
- Dividing 50 billion USD by 53 billion XRP would give an estimated price of 0.94 USD per XRP.
- The market cap would be around 50 billion USD.

4. Derivatives Markets

The derivatives market has substantial global activity, with an estimated daily trading volume reaching into the trillions of dollars. For simplicity, we assume a trading volume of about 2 trillion USD.

- **If XRP captures 10% of the derivatives market:**
    - 10% of 2 trillion USD is approximately 200 billion USD.
    - Dividing 200 billion USD by 53 billion XRP would yield an estimated price of 3.77 USD per XRP.
    - The market cap would be about 200 billion USD.
- **If XRP captures 50% of the derivatives market:**
    - 50% of 2 trillion USD would be around 1 trillion USD.
    - Dividing 1 trillion USD by 53 billion XRP would yield an estimated price of 18.87 USD per XRP.
    - The market cap would be about 1 trillion USD.

5. Bond Markets

The global bond market processes large volumes daily, with trading estimated at 700 billion to 1 trillion USD. We'll use the lower estimate for this calculation.

- **If XRP captures 10% of the bond market:**

- 10% of 700 billion USD is approximately 70 billion USD.
- Dividing 70 billion USD by 53 billion XRP would result in an estimated price of 1.32 USD per XRP.
- The market cap would be about 70 billion USD.
- **If XRP captures 50% of the bond market**:
  - 50% of 700 billion USD would be approximately 350 billion USD.
  - Dividing 350 billion USD by 53 billion XRP would yield an estimated price of 6.60 USD per XRP.
  - The market cap would be around 350 billion USD.

Summary of Potential XRP Market Caps by Sector

Market	10% Capture	50% Capture
Forex Market	660 billion USD	3.3 trillion USD
Stock Markets	50 billion USD	250 billion USD
Commodity Markets	10 billion USD	50 billion USD
Derivatives Markets	200 billion USD	1 trillion USD
Bond Markets	70 billion USD	350 billion USD

Conclusion

If XRP were to capture between 10% and 50% of the daily transaction volumes across these global markets, it would see significant increases in market cap:

- **At a 10% capture rate**, XRP's market cap could range from 10 billion USD in the commodity market to 660 billion USD in the Forex market.
- **At a 50% capture rate**, XRP's market cap could range

from 50 billion USD in the commodity market to 3.3 trillion USD in the Forex market.

This exercise highlights the potential for XRP's valuation if it were widely adopted as a bridge currency in these high-volume markets.

Comprehensive Market Cap

and Price Projections for XRP Including All Markets

By combining SWIFT and non-SWIFT international trade volumes with the Forex, stock, commodity, derivatives, and bond markets, we can estimate XRP's potential market cap under different adoption scenarios.

Total Estimated Daily Transaction Volumes Across All Markets

Market	Daily Transaction Volume (USD)
Forex Market	6.6 trillion USD
Stock Markets	500 billion USD
Commodity Markets	100 billion USD
Derivatives Markets	2 trillion USD
Bond Markets	700 billion USD
SWIFT	21 trillion USD
Non-SWIFT International Trade	48.22 billion USD

Total Daily Transaction Volume Across All Markets = 6.6 trillion + 500 billion + 100 billion + 2 trillion + 700 billion + 21 trillion + 48.22 billion = 30.948 trillion USD.

Projection at 10% Market Capture Including All Markets

If XRP captures 10% of the total daily transaction volume across all markets:

1. **Transaction Value Captured**: 10% of 30.948 trillion USD = 3.0948 trillion USD.
2. **Estimated Price per XRP**:

- Dividing 3.0948 trillion USD by the circulating supply of 53 billion XRP gives an estimated price of approximately 58.39 USD per XRP.

3. **Hypothetical Market Cap at 10% Capture**: 3.0948 trillion USD.

Projection at 50% Market Capture Including All Markets

If XRP captures 50% of the total daily transaction volume across all markets:

1. **Transaction Value Captured**: 50% of 30.948 trillion USD = 15.474 trillion USD.

2. **Estimated Price per XRP**:
   - Dividing 15.474 trillion USD by 53 billion XRP yields an estimated price of approximately 291.96 USD per XRP.

3. **Hypothetical Market Cap at 50% Capture**: 15.474 trillion USD.

Summary of XRP Market Cap and Price Projections for Combined Markets Including SWIFT and International Trade

Capture Rate	Total Transaction Value Captured	Price per XRP	Market Cap (USD)
10%	3.0948 trillion USD	58.39 USD	3.0948 trillion USD
50%	15.474 trillion USD	291.96 USD	15.474 trillion USD

Conclusion

If XRP were to capture a portion of the combined transaction volumes across all major financial markets—including SWIFT and international trade—the potential market cap and price could reach extraordinary levels:

- **At a 10% capture rate**, XRP's market cap could reach approximately **3.0948 trillion USD**, with an estimated price of **58.39 USD per XRP**.

- **At a 50% capture rate**, XRP's market cap could rise to **15.474 trillion USD**, with an estimated price of **291.96 USD per XRP**.

These projections demonstrate the high potential value XRP could achieve if widely adopted across various financial sectors, solidifying its role as a bridge currency in global transactions.

More Financial Sectors

XRP has the potential to be used in a variety of other financial sectors beyond those we've covered. Here are some additional areas where XRP could be applied to facilitate transactions and streamline processes, particularly in real estate, remittances, insurance, and supply chain finance.

1. Real Estate Transactions

The real estate market is one of the largest global asset classes, valued at around **$326 trillion USD** globally as of recent estimates. XRP could play a role in real estate transactions in several ways:

- **Cross-Border Property Transactions**: XRP can enable fast and low-cost cross-border payments, which is beneficial in international property purchases. By using XRP as a bridge currency, buyers and sellers from different countries can reduce currency conversion fees and accelerate the transfer of funds.

- **Tokenized Real Estate Assets**: Tokenizing real estate allows for fractional ownership of properties, making real estate investment more accessible. XRP could facilitate the purchase, sale, and transfer of tokenized real estate assets across platforms.

Potential Market Impact: Even a small percentage capture in real estate transactions could add substantial value to XRP's market cap due to the high value of property assets globally.

2. Remittances and Cross-Border Payments

Global remittance flows are significant, with the **World Bank estimating over $700 billion USD** in cross-border remittances annually. XRP, with its quick settlement times and low transaction costs, is particularly well-suited for the remittance market, where fees can be prohibitively high and transaction times lengthy.

- **Reduction in Fees**: XRP can cut down the fees typically associated with remittances, making it a cost-effective option for international money transfers.
- **Enhanced Reach in Emerging Markets**: Many remittance corridors serve countries with underdeveloped banking infrastructure. XRP can offer these regions an efficient means to access international payments, supporting financial inclusion.

Potential Market Impact: Capturing even a fraction of the remittance market could significantly bolster XRP's value due to the high transaction volume and demand for low-cost solutions.

3. Insurance Industry

The insurance industry, worth over **$6 trillion USD** annually, involves high volumes of payments, claims processing, and cross-border reinsurance transactions. XRP could streamline the insurance payment infrastructure by providing faster, more transparent, and lower-cost transactions.

- **Claims Settlement**: XRP could facilitate the quick settlement of insurance claims, reducing the time taken to pay out claims to policyholders.
- **Cross-Border Reinsurance Payments**: Reinsurance companies, which provide insurance for insurers, often operate globally. XRP could help reduce the transaction fees and time for these cross-border payments, enhancing the efficiency of the reinsurance process.

Potential Market Impact: By capturing a portion of the insurance transaction volume, XRP could gain traction within a high-value sector that demands efficient, transparent transactions.

4. Supply Chain Finance and Trade Finance

The supply chain finance sector helps bridge the cash flow gap between suppliers and buyers, valued at an estimated **$6 trillion USD** in trade finance annually. Trade finance, meanwhile, is a broader market supporting international trade, and is often slowed down by complex, multi-party transactions.

- **Faster Payments Across Supply Chains**: XRP can expedite payments within supply chains, ensuring that suppliers receive payment quickly, even when multiple intermediaries are involved.
- **Reduced Costs in Trade Finance**: Trade finance requires extensive paperwork and multiple currency exchanges. XRP's interoperability could reduce exchange fees and the need for intermediaries, helping companies better manage their cash flow.

Potential Market Impact: Integrating XRP in supply chain finance and trade finance could reduce payment delays, lower costs, and offer transparency, making it attractive in global trade networks.

5. Capital Markets and Securities Settlement

The global capital markets, which include equities, bonds, and other securities, are vast, with daily trading volumes in the **hundreds of billions to trillions of USD**. Securities transactions often take days to settle, tying up capital and increasing counterparty risk.

- **Instant Settlement for Securities**: XRP could enable real-time, or near-instant, settlement for securities, reducing the need for intermediaries and minimizing settlement risks.
- **Tokenized Securities**: With the rise of tokenization, traditional securities like stocks and bonds are being digitized. XRP could play a role in facilitating the transfer and settlement of these tokenized assets, especially in cross-border scenarios.

Potential Market Impact: Given the size of global capital markets, even a small market share could bring significant value to XRP, making it a viable asset for high-volume securities transactions.

6. E-commerce and Micropayments

The global e-commerce market has been growing rapidly, with sales projected to reach **$6.3 trillion USD** in 2023. XRP's low transaction fees and quick processing times make it an attractive option for e-commerce payments, especially for cross-border purchases.

- **Cross-Border E-commerce Payments**: XRP can help e-commerce platforms facilitate quick and cost-effective international transactions, reducing delays and currency conversion costs for cross-border sales.
- **Micropayments**: XRP's low transaction costs make it suitable for micropayments, allowing platforms to support smaller transactions that are typically cost-prohibitive with traditional payment processors.

Potential Market Impact: Widespread adoption in e-commerce and micropayments would expand XRP's use cases significantly, especially as online shopping and digital goods purchases continue to grow globally.

7. Decentralized Finance (DeFi)

DeFi has rapidly grown in popularity, with billions in assets locked across decentralized platforms. XRP can be integrated into DeFi ecosystems to facilitate low-cost lending, borrowing, and liquidity provision.

- **Cross-Chain Payments**: XRP could serve as a bridge asset within multi-chain DeFi ecosystems, enabling assets to move seamlessly across different blockchains.
- **Liquidity Provision**: DeFi platforms often need liquidity for lending pools. XRP, with its established liquidity and low fees, could be an attractive option for DeFi platforms seeking interoperability and cost efficiency.

Potential Market Impact: Integrating XRP with DeFi would expand its functionality beyond traditional finance, tapping into a sector valued at tens of billions and growing rapidly.

Conclusion: Expanded Market Potential for XRP

In addition to the major financial markets we previously discussed, XRP's application across these additional sectors could add significant value. By capturing even a fraction of each, XRP's role as a bridge asset could extend across nearly all forms of financial transactions, from real estate and insurance to trade finance and DeFi.

Hypothetical Market Cap

Here's a chart projecting XRP's hypothetical market cap and price if it were to capture various percentages (10% and 50%) of all discussed markets, including SWIFT transactions, international trade, Forex, stocks, commodities, derivatives, bonds, real estate, remittances, insurance, supply chain finance, capital markets, e-commerce, and DeFi. This chart will help illustrate XRP's potential valuation across multiple sectors if it gains widespread adoption.

Total Estimated Daily Transaction Volume Across All Markets

Here's a summary of the estimated daily transaction volume for each market:

Market	Estimated Daily Transaction Volume (USD)
Forex Market	6.6 trillion USD
Stock Markets	500 billion USD
Commodity Markets	100 billion USD
Derivatives Markets	2 trillion USD
Bond Markets	700 billion USD
SWIFT	21 trillion USD
Non-SWIFT International Trade	48.22 billion USD
Real Estate Transactions	1 trillion USD (approximate, cross-border)
Remittances	2 billion USD
Insurance	1 trillion USD

Market	Estimated Daily Transaction Volume (USD)
Supply Chain & Trade Finance	16.5 billion USD
Capital Markets	600 billion USD
E-commerce & Micropayments	25 billion USD
DeFi & Decentralized Markets	10 billion USD

Total Estimated Daily Transaction Volume Across All Markets = **33.80972 trillion USD.**

Projection at 10% Market Capture Across All Markets

If XRP captures 10% of the total daily transaction volume across all markets:

1. **Transaction Value Captured**: 10% of 33.80972 trillion USD = 3.380972 trillion USD.

2. **Estimated Price per XRP**:
   - Dividing 3.380972 trillion USD by the circulating supply of 53 billion XRP gives an estimated price of approximately 63.79 USD per XRP.

3. **Hypothetical Market Cap at 10% Capture**: 3.380972 trillion USD.

Projection at 50% Market Capture Across All Markets

If XRP captures 50% of the total daily transaction volume across all markets:

1. **Transaction Value Captured**: 50% of 33.80972 trillion USD = 16.90486 trillion USD.

2. **Estimated Price per XRP**:

- Dividing 16.90486 trillion USD by 53 billion XRP yields an estimated price of approximately 318.96 USD per XRP.

3. **Hypothetical Market Cap at 50% Capture**: 16.90486 trillion USD.

Summary Chart of XRP Market Cap and Price Projections Across All Markets

Capture Rate	Total Transaction Value Captured (USD)	Price per XRP (USD)	Hypothetical Market Cap (USD)
10%	3.380972 trillion	63.79	3.380972 trillion
50%	16.90486 trillion	318.96	16.90486 trillion

Conclusion

This chart demonstrates XRP's market cap potential when capturing a range of percentages across numerous global financial sectors. With comprehensive adoption, XRP could potentially achieve:

- **At 10% capture**, an estimated market cap of **3.380972 trillion USD** and a price of **63.79 USD per XRP**.
- **At 50% capture**, a market cap of **16.90486 trillion USD** with a price of **318.96 USD per XRP**.

These projections illustrate the immense growth potential XRP could experience if it becomes widely used across all major financial markets, facilitating transactions in Forex, SWIFT, international trade, real estate, and more.

Key Factors Affecting XRP's Potential Value

1. **Level of Adoption**: XRP's value would be driven primarily by adoption levels across multiple sectors. Adoption rates of even 1% to 10% in large markets like Forex, remittances, and international trade would drive substantial demand.

2. **Utility in Cross-Border Payments**: XRP's speed and low transaction cost make it ideal for cross-border and cross-currency transactions. As traditional financial institutions, SWIFT, and international remittances increasingly digitize, XRP could play a pivotal role.

3. **Token Supply Constraints**: With a fixed supply of 100 billion tokens (53 billion in circulation), increased demand would likely lead to higher valuations due to scarcity and deflationary effects from XRP's burn mechanism.

Projected Value Scenarios for XRP

Considering the diverse markets where XRP could have a role and the varying levels of adoption, here's a projection across conservative, moderate, and optimistic scenarios.

1. Conservative Scenario (1% Adoption)

If XRP captures **1%** of the total daily transaction volume across the combined markets we've discussed (33.8 trillion USD), this adoption level would still be impactful.

- **Transaction Volume Captured**: 1% of 33.8 trillion USD = 338 billion USD.

- **Estimated Price per XRP**:
    - Dividing 338 billion USD by the circulating supply of 53 billion XRP gives an approximate price of **6.38 USD per XRP**.

- **Hypothetical Market Cap**: 338 billion USD.

2. Moderate Scenario (5% Adoption)

With **5% adoption**, XRP would see a stronger presence in major markets like cross-border payments, remittances, and certain segments of capital markets and trade finance.

- **Transaction Volume Captured**: 5% of 33.8 trillion USD = 1.69 trillion USD.
- **Estimated Price per XRP**:
  - Dividing 1.69 trillion USD by the circulating supply of 53 billion XRP yields an approximate price of **31.88 USD per XRP**.
- **Hypothetical Market Cap**: 1.69 trillion USD.

3. Optimistic Scenario (15% Adoption)

If XRP achieves **15% adoption** in these markets, we could expect widespread use in SWIFT, Forex, cross-border trade, and potentially tokenized real estate and capital markets.

- **Transaction Volume Captured**: 15% of 33.8 trillion USD = 5.07 trillion USD.
- **Estimated Price per XRP**:
  - Dividing 5.07 trillion USD by 53 billion XRP yields an approximate price of **95.66 USD per XRP**.
- **Hypothetical Market Cap**: 5.07 trillion USD.

Final Overview of XRP Potential Value Projections

Scenario	Total Transaction Value Captured (USD)	Price per XRP (USD)	Hypothetical Market Cap (USD)
Conservative (1%)	338 billion USD	6.38	338 billion USD
Moderate (5%)	1.69 trillion USD	31.88	1.69 trillion USD

Scenario	Total Transaction Value Captured (USD)	Price per XRP (USD)	Hypothetical Market Cap (USD)
Optimistic (15%)	5.07 trillion USD	95.66	5.07 trillion USD

Conclusion: Potential Value of XRP

Based on these projections, XRP's potential value could range from **6.38 USD in a conservative adoption scenario** to **95.66 USD in an optimistic scenario**. The most likely outcomes lie within these bounds, driven by adoption in the global financial ecosystem and XRP's ability to meet the needs of cross-border payments, remittances, and other transaction-heavy industries.

While these projections are speculative, they reflect XRP's theoretical value based on widespread adoption in financial markets, highlighting its potential if it becomes a critical component of global finance.

$1,000 XRP?

The idea of XRP reaching $1,000 per token is certainly ambitious and would imply XRP capturing a substantial share of the world's financial transactions. Achieving this price would require extraordinary levels of adoption and integration across many global financial systems and markets. Here's a breakdown of what would need to happen for XRP to reach such a valuation, along with some realistic considerations.

What $1,000 per XRP Would Imply

1. **Total Market Cap**: With a circulating supply of approximately 53 billion XRP, a $1,000 valuation per XRP would give it a market cap of **$53 trillion USD**. For context, that's more than twice the size of the U.S. GDP and greater than the total global stock market capitalization, which is around $100 trillion.

2. **Market Capture Requirements**: To support a $1,000 valuation, XRP would likely need to capture significant market share across the following:

   - **Global Payment Systems**: SWIFT and other cross-border payment systems would need to fully adopt XRP.

   - **Forex Market**: XRP would need to handle a substantial volume of Forex transactions, which averages $6.6 trillion per day.

   - **Real Estate and Trade Finance**: XRP would need to facilitate large segments of international trade and potentially tokenized real estate transactions.

   - **Banking and Remittances**: XRP would need widespread adoption across international remittance platforms and be used as a primary asset by major banks for liquidity and cross-border payments.

3. **Global Financial Infrastructure Shift**: XRP reaching $1,000 would imply a transformative shift in the global financial infrastructure, with traditional financial systems heavily adopting blockchain solutions for cost savings, speed, and efficiency.

Challenges to a $1,000 Valuation

1. **Regulatory Adoption and Clarity**: For XRP to achieve this level of market dominance, regulatory acceptance worldwide would be essential. XRP would need to be recognized as a standard currency or liquidity tool, which could face challenges, particularly in markets with regulatory concerns around crypto assets.

2. **Competition from Other Cryptocurrencies and Digital Assets**: Many blockchain projects are competing for similar use cases (e.g., cross-border payments and trade finance), including stablecoins and central bank digital currencies (CBDCs). XRP would need to outperform these alternatives or coexist alongside them in a unique role.

3. **Utility Demand vs. Speculative Demand**: At present, a large portion of XRP's value comes from speculative demand. For XRP to reach $1,000, the demand would need to shift significantly toward **utility-driven demand**, where XRP is used daily in high-volume transactions across multiple sectors.

4. **Liquidity Constraints**: A $1,000 price would require enough liquidity to support transactions on this scale without causing volatility. This level of liquidity could be challenging without deep institutional support and very high daily transaction volumes.

Realistic Potential: Is $1,000 Feasible?

While a $1,000 price tag for XRP is theoretically possible if it were to become a global settlement currency across many financial sectors, it would be a massive leap from current valuations. The most realistic path to such a valuation would involve:

- **Extensive Institutional Adoption**: XRP would need to be adopted not only by banks and payment providers but also by other industries at a massive scale.
- **Global Standardization**: XRP would have to be accepted as a standard bridge currency for international trade, real estate, and other high-value transactions.
- **Market Stability and Liquidity**: Significant investment in infrastructure to support XRP's liquidity and prevent high volatility would be required, likely through partnerships with large financial institutions and central banks.

Realistic Projections

A more feasible long-term valuation, based on today's understanding of adoption trends, regulatory challenges, and market needs, could range between **$10 and $100** if XRP becomes widely used in cross-border payments, remittances, and select financial markets. However, achieving $1,000 would require unprecedented levels of adoption, market integration, and global regulatory support.

In summary, while $1,000 per XRP is not impossible, it is extremely ambitious and would require a major evolution in global finance with XRP at the center. The current outlook suggests more modest price projections are realistic, with higher valuations contingent on extensive, utility-driven adoption.

XRP $2700+ but HOW?

Asset Backed Cryptos

The concept of the Quantum Financial System (QFS), as discussed in various speculative theories, envisions a future financial infrastructure where digital assets like XRP and XLM are linked to precious metals such as gold and silver. This idea suggests that specific cryptocurrencies would be pegged to the values of these metals, acting as digital representations of tangible assets and adding a layer of stability and intrinsic value.

Key Points on QFS and Asset-Backed Cryptos

1. **XRP as a Gold-Equivalent**: In the QFS, XRP is proposed to serve as a "digital gold" standard. This means that one unit of XRP would hold a value equivalent to one ounce of gold, theoretically stabilizing its price and creating a direct link between XRP and gold's market value. Advocates of this model suggest that the stability from gold backing would enable XRP to function as a global bridge currency, especially in cross-border payments.

2. **XLM as a Silver-Equivalent**: Similarly, **Stellar Lumens (XLM)** is often described as representing "digital silver." This concept positions XLM as a cryptocurrency for lower-value, day-to-day transactions, given silver's traditionally lower value compared to gold. In the QFS, XLM could act as a stable, lower-value currency supporting microtransactions and remittances.

3. **The QFS's Asset-Backed Vision**: The Quantum Financial System theorizes a blockchain-based, secure, and transparent financial network that aims to replace fiat-based financial systems with asset-backed currencies. Cryptocurrencies like XRP and XLM, if pegged to precious metals, would purportedly facilitate fair and equitable global transactions by eliminating inflationary pressures associated with fiat currencies.

4. **Current Market Realities**: It's essential to note that this vision remains speculative and has not been implemented by central banks or financial authorities. No official entity has confirmed a direct linkage between XRP, XLM, or any other cryptocurrency with physical gold or silver. The current use cases for XRP and XLM focus primarily on cross-border payments and low-fee transactions, not on precious metal backing.

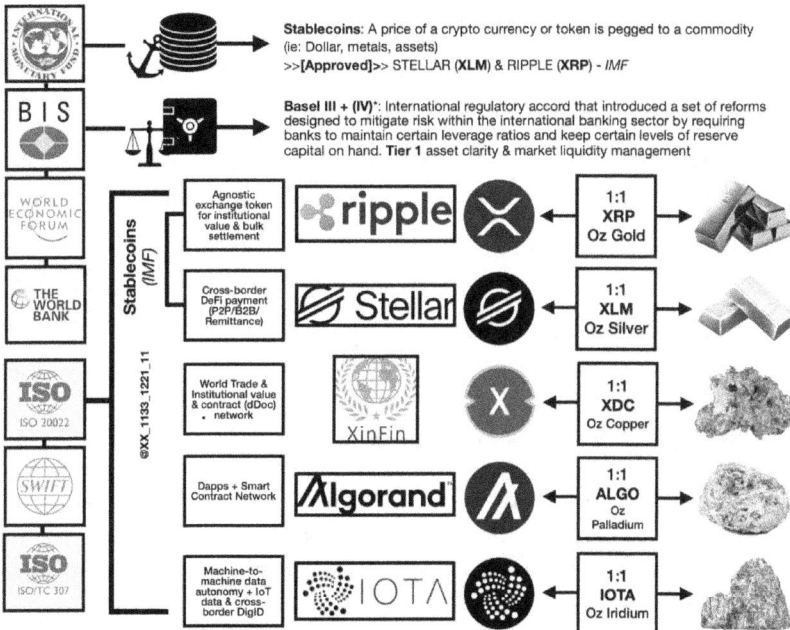

More about this available in NESARA/GESARA: and the Quantum Financial System by Bruce Goldwell.

If XRP were to be backed by gold, with each unit pegged to the value of one ounce of gold, its price would theoretically align with the current spot price of gold. Given today's gold price of approximately $2,700 per ounce, this model would position XRP at a value of $2,700 per token. This would represent a dramatic increase from current market levels, transforming XRP into an asset with intrinsic value tied directly to a physical commodity. Such a structure could bring unprecedented stability and investor confidence, as it would align XRP with the long-standing stability and scarcity of gold. However, for this to be viable, a substantial reserve of gold would need to be maintained to back the circulating supply of XRP, along with mechanisms to regulate its value reliably. This peg could redefine XRP's role in the financial ecosystem, making it a potential cornerstone of asset-backed digital currencies in the Quantum Financial System (QFS) or similar models.

Challenges to Implementation

For XRP or XLM to be pegged to gold or silver, significant market and regulatory changes would need to occur:

- **Regulatory Approval**: The QFS would require widespread government adoption and regulatory restructuring, particularly with respect to asset-backed digital currencies.

- **Liquidity and Stability**: Pegging XRP or XLM to physical assets would require substantial reserves of gold and silver to maintain stability and provide liquidity, which could be challenging at a global scale.

- **Market Mechanisms**: To maintain the peg, mechanisms for minting, redemption, and liquidation would be required, along with policies ensuring each crypto unit can reliably equate to an ounce of gold (or silver for XLM).

For more about the Quantum Financial System and the prospect of Cryptocurrencies being backed by gold, silver and other assets see **NESARA/GESARA: and the Quantum Financial System by Bruce Goldwell, https://amzn.to/4hzDWZh**

In summary, while the QFS and the idea of asset-backed cryptocurrencies offer an intriguing perspective on the future of digital finance, they currently reside within speculative and theoretical frameworks. However, the idea continues to interest segments of the crypto community, including the "XRP Army" and others who see XRP and XLM as future standards for a more stable and secure global financial system.

How to Get Started with XRP

If you want to position yourself before the rest of the world catches on, here's exactly how I got started:

- **Create your free Uphold account**
    - https://bit.ly/FreeUpholdAcct
- **Set up your Chime account** (or use your current bank or card)
    - https://bit.ly/ChimeXRPGateway
- **Link your Chime card or bank account** to Uphold.
- **Load funds**—whether $20 or $1,000, start where you're comfortable.
- **Buy XRP**—as simple as that.
- **Withdraw when needed** by transferring back to your card or account.

These are my personal referral links. They don't cost you a penny but connect you directly to the same setup I use to build my long-term crypto position.

BONUS MATERIAL

The Trump Effect
Awakening America to Truth, Trust, and Financial Prosperity

Bruce Goldwell

Copyright © 2024-2025 by Bruce Goldwell
All rights reserved.

No part of this book may be reproduced, distributed, or transmitted in any form or by any means, including photocopying, recording, or other electronic or mechanical methods, without the prior written permission of the publisher, except in the case of brief quotations embodied in critical reviews and certain other noncommercial uses permitted by copyright law. For permission requests, write to the publisher at the address below.

Disclaimer

This book is provided for informational and educational purposes only. The author does not intend to offer financial, legal, or investment advice. All information, analysis, and opinions expressed in this book are based on the author's research and personal views as of the date of publication.

Readers are encouraged to conduct their own research and seek the guidance of a qualified financial advisor or investment professional before making any financial decisions. The author and publisher expressly disclaim any liability for any direct or indirect loss or risk incurred as a result of the information provided in this book.

This book should not be considered a recommendation to buy, sell, or hold any specific investment or asset, nor does it endorse any specific cryptocurrency or financial instrument.

Preface

Awakening to Truth, Sovereignty, and a New Financial Future

We live in extraordinary times. In an era where narratives flood every channel and platform, the line between truth and manipulation has been deliberately blurred. Institutions once trusted to inform and protect now often serve as engines of persuasion—distorting facts to influence minds, suppress dissent, and maintain control.

Few individuals have exposed this agenda more clearly than Donald J. Trump. His presidency not only triggered a media firestorm—it ripped the mask off a carefully guarded globalist machine. From smear campaigns and fake news to psychological warfare and censorship, the efforts to silence and discredit him reveal the stakes of a much larger battle: **the future of national sovereignty in an age of global manipulation.**

But something powerful has emerged from this chaos: **an awakening.** Millions across the United States—and beyond—began to question official stories, challenge media narratives, and search for truth on their own terms. This awakening transcends political identity. It is a rebirth of discernment, a hunger for results over rhetoric, and a return to trust in that which is real, principled, and proven.

The Importance of Truth in a Collapsing Global Order

While Trump has been confronting this system in the public eye, another revolution has been taking shape—quietly, but no less world-shifting. Behind the scenes, **a new financial architecture** is emerging, powered by blockchain technology and ISO 20022-compliant assets like **XRP and XLM**. These aren't just cryptocurrencies—they are **the foundation of a new, decentralized financial world**.

Together, these two awakenings—**truth and sovereignty on one side, financial liberation on the other—are part of the same historical shift**:

- From centralized control to distributed empowerment.
- From globalist dependency to national and individual sovereignty.
- From economic servitude to opportunity for all.

Trump's economic policies, peace-first foreign doctrine, and rejection of perpetual war all point to a deeper objective: to **dismantle the postwar imperial system** and rebuild a world of sovereign partnerships, honest trade, and financial transparency.

A Call to Readers: Question Everything, Act Now

This is not just a book about Donald Trump.
It's not just about blockchain or crypto.

It's a call to **awaken, think, and act**. It is a roadmap for those who feel something is broken—but believe it can still be repaired.

You are called to:

- **Think Critically** – In a world of scripted narratives, truth requires effort. Always ask: *Who benefits from this story?*
- **Demand Results** – Empty promises change nothing. Judge leaders by what they *do*, not what they say.
- **Seize the Financial Moment** – The ISO 20022 shift is a rare, generational opportunity. XRP, XLM, and other compliant assets are not trends—they are tools for liberation.

The Trump Effect: Sovereignty, Truth, and Prosperity

This book is not partisan. It is not blind praise.
It is about **results that exposed an empire**, leadership that defied manipulation, and a vision that placed America—and the average citizen—back at the center of power.

We stand at a crossroads:

4. **One path leads to digital serfdom, narrative control, and centralized surveillance.**

5. **The other leads to truth, sovereignty, and financial independence.**

This book invites you to take the second path—to join those who are awake, aware, and ready to reshape the future.

Welcome to **The Trump Effect: Awakening America to Truth, Trust, and Financial Prosperity.**
Let's begin the journey together.

Part I: Understanding the Tools of Manipulation

Chapter 1: The Anatomy of Propaganda
What is Propaganda?

Propaganda is the deliberate and systematic dissemination of information, ideas, or rumors designed to influence opinions, emotions, or behaviors. It is often biased, misleading, or outright false, crafted to advance a particular agenda or cause. Unlike straightforward communication, propaganda manipulates facts to evoke specific reactions and align individuals with a specific ideology or narrative.

Propaganda can take many forms—posters, speeches, films, news reports, and social media campaigns. It is not a new phenomenon; throughout history, leaders, governments, and organizations have used propaganda to rally support, demonize opponents, or justify controversial actions.

Historical Examples of Propaganda

4. **World War I and II**: Nations on both sides of the conflicts used propaganda to bolster morale, dehumanize enemies, and encourage enlistment. Posters like "Uncle Sam Wants You" and films depicting enemy nations as barbaric were widespread.

5. **Nazi Germany**: Under Joseph Goebbels, the Ministry of Propaganda used films, speeches, and newspapers to push antisemitic rhetoric and fuel nationalism, ultimately enabling the atrocities of the Holocaust.

6. **The Cold War**: The United States and the Soviet Union engaged in propaganda battles to promote their ideologies—democracy versus communism. Campaigns framed the other side as existential threats to freedom and security.

7. **Modern Day Examples**: Today, propaganda is often subtler and disseminated through digital channels, using

algorithms and targeted ads to reach specific demographics.

How It Applies to Modern Media

While historical propaganda was overt and easily recognizable, modern propaganda often disguises itself as news, entertainment, or social discourse. Media outlets—whether intentionally or inadvertently—play a key role in amplifying narratives that align with specific agendas.

Techniques include:

- **Selective storytelling**: Highlighting certain facts while ignoring others to shape a specific perspective.
- **Emotional appeals**: Using fear, anger, or hope to bypass rational analysis.
- **Repetition**: Repeating a false narrative so frequently that it begins to feel true (e.g., "Russia Collusion").
- **Censorship**: Silencing dissenting voices under the guise of combating misinformation.

Real Examples of Selective Storytelling to Manipulate Public Opinion

- **The Russia Collusion Narrative**:
    - For years, mainstream media pushed the idea that Donald Trump colluded with Russia to win the 2016 election. Despite a lengthy investigation and no evidence proving collusion, the narrative persisted, damaging public trust and Trump's presidency.
- **The Charlottesville Hoax**:
    - Media outlets selectively edited Trump's comments about the Charlottesville incident, claiming he called white supremacists "fine people." In reality,

Trump explicitly condemned neo-Nazis and white nationalists, but the full statement was omitted to fit a divisive narrative.

- **January 6: Insurrection or Protest?**
    - The events of January 6, 2021, were framed as an "insurrection" despite lacking evidence of an organized coup. Key details, such as unarmed protestors and Capitol security failures, were downplayed while the narrative of a violent uprising dominated headlines.
- **Censorship of the Hunter Biden Laptop Story**:
    - In the lead-up to the 2020 election, major media platforms dismissed the Hunter Biden laptop story as "Russian disinformation." Only later did it emerge that the story was legitimate, yet the suppression of this information influenced voters.

Conclusion: Recognizing Modern Propaganda

Propaganda has evolved, but its purpose remains the same: to manipulate opinions and behaviors. By understanding its methods and recognizing its presence in modern media, readers can arm themselves with the tools needed to critically evaluate the information they consume. In the following chapters, we will delve deeper into the specific tactics used to influence public perception and explore the real consequences of these manipulations.

Chapter 2: Fake News and Alternative Facts

Definition and History of Fake News

Fake news refers to false or misleading information presented as legitimate news with the intent to deceive, manipulate public perception, or generate profit. While it seems like a recent phenomenon, fake news has existed for centuries. In earlier times, false pamphlets and sensationalist newspapers were used to sway public opinion or discredit political rivals. However, the rise of digital media and social platforms has amplified the spread of fake news to unprecedented levels.

- **Yellow Journalism (19th Century)**: Sensationalized stories with exaggerated or fabricated details were used to sell newspapers. This era laid the foundation for modern fake news.
- **The Internet Age**: Social media platforms, with their lack of editorial oversight, have allowed fake news to proliferate rapidly, reaching millions within hours.

Fake news today thrives on clickbait, emotional triggers, and deliberate misrepresentation. As stories go viral, false narratives often outpace the truth, leaving lasting impressions even after they are debunked.

How Mainstream Media Has Shaped Public Perception of Trump

The presidency of Donald J. Trump highlighted the power of mainstream media to shape narratives. From the outset, Trump's candidacy and presidency were met with skepticism, hostility, and a level of media scrutiny unparalleled in modern times.

4. **Negative Coverage**: Studies show that over 90% of Trump's media coverage during certain periods was negative, creating a persistent perception of chaos and controversy.
5. **Selective Reporting**: Positive achievements—such as

economic growth, record unemployment rates, and peace agreements—were often buried under headlines focused on scandals and speculation.

6. **Amplification of Unverified Claims**: Stories based on anonymous sources and unverified leaks were frequently presented as fact, influencing public opinion before the truth could emerge.

Examples of Fake Stories That Were Later Debunked

- **The Russia Collusion Hoax**:
    - For years, media outlets reported that Trump colluded with Russia to win the 2016 election. The Mueller investigation ultimately found no evidence of collusion, but the damage to Trump's reputation was significant.

- **The Fine People Hoax**:
    - Trump's comments following the Charlottesville incident were selectively edited to make it seem as though he praised white supremacists. In reality, he explicitly condemned them.

- **The Kavanaugh Accusations**:
    - During Justice Brett Kavanaugh's confirmation hearings, unsubstantiated allegations of misconduct were widely reported. Subsequent investigations found no corroborating evidence.

- **The Trump Taxes Story**:
    - Headlines claiming Trump paid no taxes often omitted the context that he had complied with existing tax laws and utilized legal deductions, as do many businesses.

Conclusion: The Lasting Impact of Fake News

Even after being debunked, fake news leaves a lasting impression on public perception. A false story can spread rapidly, while the correction—if it comes at all—receives far less attention. By critically examining the media's role in shaping narratives around Donald Trump, we can better understand how fake news influences elections, policies, and trust in leadership. In the following chapters, we will explore additional tactics used to distort truth and manipulate public perception.

Chapter 3: Gaslighting the Public

Understanding Gaslighting as a Psychological Tool

Gaslighting is a form of psychological manipulation in which individuals or groups are made to doubt their perceptions, memories, or understanding of reality. This tactic creates confusion and disorientation, ultimately leading people to question what they know to be true. While gaslighting often occurs in personal relationships, it is increasingly used in political and media discourse to distort the truth and influence public opinion.

Gaslighting operates by:

- **Denial of Evidence**: Dismissing or outright denying facts that are verifiable.
- **Repetition of Falsehoods**: Repeating untrue statements until they are accepted as fact.
- **Blame Shifting**: Accusing others of dishonesty or wrongdoing to deflect scrutiny.
- **Creating Confusion**: Flooding the public with contradictory information to obscure the truth.

By employing these techniques, those in power can manipulate public perception, erode trust in reliable information, and control the narrative.

How January 6 Was Framed as an Insurrection Despite Contradictory Evidence

The events of January 6, 2021, at the U.S. Capitol were quickly labeled an "insurrection" by politicians and mainstream media. This framing painted the protest as a coordinated coup attempt, a claim that many accepted without question. However, upon closer examination, key details emerged that contradicted this narrative:

- **Unarmed Protestors**: Despite claims of a violent insurrection, most participants were unarmed and did not engage in planned violence.

- **Security Failures**: Capitol security was overwhelmed, but questions remain about why reinforcements were not preemptively deployed despite intelligence warnings.
- **Selective Footage**: Media outlets focused on the most chaotic and extreme images while ignoring peaceful protestors or other aspects of the day.
- **Lack of Coordination**: Investigations found no evidence of an organized plan to overthrow the government.

The gaslighting surrounding January 6 fostered fear and division, encouraging the public to accept the narrative without questioning inconsistencies. This deliberate manipulation served to demonize political opponents and distract from other pressing issues.

The Emotional and Psychological Impact of Manipulated Narratives on Voters

The relentless gaslighting by politicians and media has far-reaching consequences for individuals and society as a whole:

- **Erosion of Trust**: When people are repeatedly told conflicting information, they lose trust in all sources of information, fostering skepticism and cynicism.
- **Emotional Manipulation**: Fear, anger, and guilt are exploited to push specific agendas, leaving voters emotionally drained and divided.
- **Decision Paralysis**: Conflicting narratives create confusion, making it harder for individuals to make informed decisions.
- **Demonization of Dissent**: Those who question mainstream narratives are labeled as extremists or conspiracy theorists, silencing legitimate debate.

Gaslighting does not merely distort the truth—it reshapes perceptions, emotions, and decision-making. By understanding these tactics, readers can recognize manipulation, demand accountability, and reclaim their ability to think independently.

Conclusion: Exposing the Gaslighting

January 6 serves as a powerful example of how gaslighting can shape public perception and stoke division. By examining the inconsistencies and contradictions in the official narrative, we can better understand how gaslighting operates in political discourse. In the following chapters, we will continue to expose other manipulative tactics used to influence the public and explore their real-world consequences.

Chapter 4: The Art of the Smear Campaign

What is a Smear Campaign?

A smear campaign is a deliberate effort to damage someone's reputation through false, exaggerated, or misleading information. Typically used in politics, smear campaigns rely on personal attacks, unsubstantiated allegations, and relentless repetition to create doubt and suspicion. The goal is not necessarily to prove wrongdoing but to tarnish an individual's image so profoundly that public trust is irreparably damaged.

Smear campaigns often include:

- **Anonymous Sources**: Using unnamed individuals to spread damaging claims without accountability.
- **Selective Reporting**: Highlighting only negative or out-of-context information while ignoring exculpatory facts.
- **Amplification**: Repeating accusations across multiple platforms to make them appear credible.
- **Emotional Appeals**: Evoking outrage, disgust, or fear to bypass rational analysis.

How Smear Campaigns Were Used Against Trump

Donald Trump's presidency was marked by an unprecedented level of personal and professional attacks. Media outlets, political opponents, and activists often employed smear tactics to undermine his credibility, delegitimize his achievements, and sway public opinion. Key examples include:

6. **The Steele Dossier**:
    1. The Steele dossier, a collection of unverified claims about Trump's ties to Russia, was widely reported as fact. Despite its lack of corroboration, the dossier fueled the Russia collusion narrative and dominated headlines for months.
7. **Accusations of Racism**:

1. Trump's statements were often taken out of context or misrepresented to paint him as a racist. For instance, his comments on illegal immigration were twisted to imply he called all Mexicans "rapists" when he was specifically addressing criminal elements.

8. **The Impeachment Trials**:
   1. Trump's impeachment proceedings were based on allegations that were later found to lack sufficient evidence. However, the damage to his reputation had already been done, as the media amplified the accusations relentlessly.

9. **Personal Attacks on Character**:
   1. From claims about his mental fitness to attacks on his family, Trump faced a barrage of personal smears designed to undermine public confidence in his leadership.

The Role of Media in Amplifying Smears

The mainstream media played a central role in amplifying smear campaigns against Trump. Techniques included:

- **Echo Chambers**: Repeating accusations across multiple outlets to create the illusion of consensus.
- **Sensationalism**: Using inflammatory language and headlines to generate outrage and clicks.
- **Failure to Correct**: Even after accusations were debunked, media outlets often failed to issue prominent corrections, allowing the smears to linger.

The Impact of Smear Campaigns on Public Perception

Smear campaigns are effective because they exploit human psychology. People are more likely to remember negative information, even if it is later proven false. The consequences of smear campaigns include:

- **Erosion of Trust**: Smears create doubt, making it harder for individuals to trust political leaders or institutions.
- **Polarization**: Smear tactics deepen divisions by reinforcing negative stereotypes and encouraging tribalism.
- **Distraction from Issues**: By focusing on personal attacks, smear campaigns divert attention from substantive policy discussions.

Conclusion: Recognizing and Resisting Smear Campaigns

Smear campaigns are a powerful tool for manipulating public opinion, but they rely on a lack of critical thinking and discernment. By understanding how smears operate and questioning the motives behind damaging accusations, readers can avoid falling prey to these tactics. In the next chapter, we will explore how emotional appeals and fearmongering are used to influence public perception and drive political agendas.

Part II: The Weaponization of Politics and Media

Chapter 5: PsyOps and Demagoguery

Psychological Operations in Shaping Public Perception

Psychological operations, commonly known as PsyOps, have been employed throughout history to manipulate public perception and influence political outcomes. During Trump's presidency, PsyOps took on a modern form, blending traditional propaganda techniques with the power of digital media, mainstream news outlets, and social platforms. These tactics were aimed at shaping opinions, fostering division, and suppressing dissent among Trump's supporters.

The Role of Fear, Anger, and Emotional Manipulation

Fear and anger are powerful tools for influencing behavior and decision-making. By framing Trump and his supporters as dangerous or extremist, opponents successfully weaponized emotions to polarize the electorate and discredit Trump's message.

- **Fear**: Narratives about Trump's policies often emphasized apocalyptic outcomes. For example, border security measures were described as harbingers of fascism, while environmental deregulation was framed as catastrophic for the planet.

- **Anger**: Media and political opponents repeatedly pointed to Trump's rhetoric as a source of division, fueling anger among groups opposed to his presidency. Selective reporting of Trump's statements further amplified public outrage.

- **Emotional Triggers**: High-profile events—such as protests, riots, or incidents involving law enforcement—were leveraged to evoke emotional responses. These events were often tied to Trump's leadership, creating a perception of chaos and instability.

For Trump supporters, this emotional warfare created an environment of defensiveness and frustration. Their beliefs and values were often vilified, leading to a "us vs. them" dynamic that further entrenched divisions.

Key Tools of Psychological Operations

- **Repetition**: The constant repetition of slogans like "Trump is a racist," "Trump is a dictator," or "Trump is a threat to democracy" created a sense of inevitability. Over time, these claims were accepted as truth, regardless of evidence.
- **Symbolism**: Imagery of protests, children in detention centers, or confrontations with law enforcement was strategically used to invoke strong emotional reactions. These visuals reinforced negative narratives without addressing the broader context.
- **Information Control**: The suppression of positive news related to Trump's administration, such as economic successes or foreign policy achievements, ensured the public remained focused on negative stories.

Demagoguery: Weaponizing Political Rhetoric to Stoke Division

Demagoguery involves the use of impassioned rhetoric, emotional appeals, and inflammatory language to rally support or opposition. During Trump's presidency, key political speeches and public statements were filled with demagoguery designed to stoke division and further polarize the nation.

Examples include:

- **Accusations of Authoritarianism**: Trump's calls for "law and order" during riots were framed as authoritarian power grabs. Politicians and media figures compared Trump to historical dictators, invoking fear and anger.
- **Racial Division**: High-profile political speeches often

accused Trump of enabling racism or white supremacy, despite a lack of evidence. These accusations served to alienate certain demographics and discredit Trump's message of national unity.

- **Class Warfare**: Trump's tax reforms and economic policies were described as benefiting only the wealthy, despite significant benefits for middle- and working-class Americans. This rhetoric fueled resentment and reinforced stereotypes about Trump's agenda.

The Media's Role in Amplifying PsyOps and Demagoguery

The media played a critical role in disseminating PsyOps and demagogic rhetoric. Selective reporting, omission of context, and sensationalism ensured that emotionally charged narratives dominated public discourse. For example:

- Statements taken out of context, such as Trump's remarks about Charlottesville, were repeated endlessly to paint him as sympathetic to extremists.
- Headlines focused on Trump's tone or language rather than the substance of his policies, creating a narrative of chaos and unfitness for office.

Impact on Trump Supporters

The constant barrage of psychological manipulation created a chilling effect on Trump supporters. Fear of social ostracization, job loss, or public backlash led many to silence their views. Trump's base was often portrayed as uneducated, bigoted, or extremist, further reinforcing negative stereotypes.

However, these tactics also had the unintended effect of galvanizing Trump's supporters. The perception of unfair treatment and manipulation deepened their loyalty, as they saw Trump as a lone figure fighting against a corrupt establishment.

Conclusion

PsyOps and demagoguery were pivotal in shaping public perception during Trump's presidency. By leveraging fear, anger, and emotional manipulation, opponents succeeded in creating a polarized and divided electorate. The media's complicity in amplifying these tactics further obscured the truth, leaving many Americans unable to engage in objective discussions about Trump's policies and achievements.

Understanding these strategies is crucial for recognizing how psychological operations and inflammatory rhetoric are used to manipulate perceptions, not just in Trump's case, but in modern political discourse as a whole.

Chapter 6: Dog Whistling and Red Herrings

Breaking Down Coded Language Used to Vilify Trump and His Policies

The term "dog whistling" refers to coded language or messages that appear innocuous on the surface but carry deeper, often controversial meanings for a particular audience. During Trump's presidency, the accusation of dog whistling became a powerful rhetorical tool to discredit him and his policies. Critics often claimed Trump's statements or policies were subtle appeals to racism, misogyny, xenophobia, or other forms of prejudice. However, these allegations frequently overshadowed substantive discussions about his achievements and the broader context of his presidency.

The Creation of Red Herrings

A red herring is a deliberate distraction or misdirection designed to pull attention away from core issues. In Trump's case, topics like racism, misogyny, and other cultural accusations became common red herrings. These narratives dominated headlines, obscuring Trump's tangible policy successes and appealing to emotional responses rather than factual analysis.

For instance, Trump's immigration policies were often described as "racist" or "xenophobic" in the media. Terms like "dog whistle" were used to suggest that his calls for border security, deportation of criminal aliens, and stricter vetting processes were covert appeals to prejudice. However, these discussions often ignored critical aspects of Trump's immigration platform, such as reducing illegal crossings, addressing human trafficking, and improving national security.

Similarly, Trump's rhetoric on economic revitalization was met with accusations of exclusion. While the administration's tax reforms and deregulation policies spurred job creation and economic growth, detractors framed these initiatives as favoring the wealthy or rooted in inequality, thus shifting the focus from their tangible results.

The Emotional Playbook: Vilification Over Verification

The framing of Trump as a figurehead for racism, misogyny, or authoritarianism became an emotional playbook. Rather than dissecting the policies themselves, narratives focused on vilifying the man behind them. This approach served two purposes: to rally opposition and to distract the public from measurable successes.

For example:

- **Racism Accusations** – Trump's statements on Charlottesville and border walls were cherry-picked or misquoted to paint him as racially divisive.

- **Misogyny Claims** – While Trump's personal remarks were criticized, initiatives like the Women's Global Development and Prosperity Initiative and historically low female unemployment rates under his administration received little media focus.

- **Islamophobia Allegations** – Trump's "travel ban" was frequently labeled as discriminatory, despite its focus on security and its grounding in concerns raised during the Obama administration.

These red herrings often amplified ideological divides, making objective conversations about policies virtually impossible. Rather than debating the effectiveness of border control, tax reforms, or deregulation, the public narrative was hijacked by emotionally charged accusations.

How Coded Language Became a Weapon

The rise of identity politics and media sensationalism transformed the term "dog whistle" into a weapon. Words or phrases used by Trump—even those with neutral intent—were interpreted as covert signals. For example, Trump's emphasis on "law and order" during nationwide riots was framed as coded language appealing to racial bias, despite its focus on restoring safety and security in communities.

Ultimately, these accusations of dog whistling became self-sustaining narratives. They distracted the public from Trump's successes in areas such as economic growth, foreign policy achievements like the Abraham Accords, and workforce empowerment initiatives.

Chapter 7: Obfuscation: Hiding the Truth

How Investigations Like the "Russia Collusion Hoax" Were Drawn Out to Obscure the Truth

The term "Russia Collusion Hoax" refers to the prolonged and heavily publicized investigation into alleged collusion between Donald Trump's campaign and Russia during the 2016 election. While this investigation dominated headlines and public discourse for years, its eventual findings revealed no conclusive evidence of collusion. The drawn-out process became a textbook example of obfuscation—a deliberate effort to muddy the waters, distract the public, and obscure the truth.

The Political Weaponization of Investigations

Investigations are meant to uncover facts, but in the case of the Russia probe, the process itself became the point of focus. From the FBI's Crossfire Hurricane to the Mueller Report, the narrative of collusion persisted despite repeated failures to produce evidence. Rather than clarifying the situation, the investigation served as a cloud of suspicion over Trump's presidency, hindering his administration's ability to focus on governance.

The role of intelligence agencies and the Department of Justice (DOJ) during this period came under scrutiny. Revelations of bias within the FBI's leadership, misuse of the Foreign Intelligence Surveillance Act (FISA) warrants, and reliance on questionable sources like the Steele Dossier raised serious questions about the integrity of the investigation. Yet, these issues were often buried under sensational headlines and partisan rhetoric.

Muddying the Waters: The Media's Role

The media played a pivotal role in perpetuating the Russia collusion narrative. Leaks from anonymous sources, selective reporting, and exaggerated claims turned the investigation into a media spectacle. Terms like "smoking gun" and "bombshell" were used repeatedly, creating an illusion of guilt that lingered despite the absence of evidence.

For example:

- Headlines speculated about secret meetings, back channels, and alleged kompromat.
- News cycles fixated on theories of collusion while ignoring exculpatory evidence.
- Figures like Adam Schiff claimed to have proof of collusion, yet such claims never materialized.

The public was left with the impression that Trump's presidency was under a dark cloud of illegitimacy, even as investigations ultimately failed to substantiate the allegations.

The Role of the DOJ and Intelligence Agencies

Beyond the Russia collusion narrative, Trump's presidency highlighted deep concerns about the politicization of the DOJ and intelligence agencies. These institutions, traditionally seen as neutral arbiters of justice, were increasingly viewed as partisan actors. The FBI's handling of the FISA process, the slow release of exonerating documents, and the selective targeting of individuals connected to Trump all fueled perceptions of a two-tiered system of justice.

Key examples include:

- The use of the unverified Steele Dossier to obtain surveillance warrants.
- Leaks of classified information to media outlets to advance political narratives.
- Unequal treatment of figures like Michael Flynn compared to others with similar allegations.

Obfuscation as a Political Strategy

The Russia collusion investigation exemplified how prolonged processes and sensational headlines can obscure the truth. By the time the Mueller Report confirmed no collusion, the damage to Trump's presidency had already been done. The lingering suspicion overshadowed policy successes, foreign diplomacy, and economic growth, creating a narrative that distracted the public from reality.

Conclusion

Obfuscation became a defining feature of Trump's presidency. Investigations like the Russia collusion probe were not merely about uncovering facts but served as tools to create doubt, suspicion, and chaos. Coupled with media complicity and the politicization of justice, these efforts successfully obscured Trump's achievements and shaped public perception in ways that were difficult to reverse.

Trump's presidency provides a case study in how investigations, media narratives, and institutional biases can be weaponized to muddy the waters. Recognizing these tactics is essential for ensuring transparency, accountability, and an informed public moving forward.

Part III: Exposing the Lies

Chapter 8: Debunking the Trump Lies

Analyzing Accusations and the Outcomes

Throughout Donald Trump's political career, critics and media outlets have perpetuated numerous accusations, which have been subjects of heated debates, investigations, and controversies. This chapter breaks down key allegations, examines their factual basis, and evaluates their outcomes.

1. The Russia Collusion Narrative

The Accusation:

One of the most significant accusations against Trump was the claim that his 2016 presidential campaign colluded with Russia to influence the election outcome. The allegation gained momentum following the release of the Steele Dossier, which contained unverified claims about Trump's connections to Russia.

Investigations and Outcomes:

- **Mueller Report:** Special Counsel Robert Mueller conducted a two-year investigation into the allegations. The report, released in 2019, concluded that while Russia did attempt to interfere in the election through misinformation campaigns and hacking operations, there was *no sufficient evidence to establish criminal conspiracy* between Trump or his campaign and the Russian government.

- **FBI Missteps:** The investigation revealed that parts of the Steele Dossier were unreliable. Additionally, the FBI's surveillance process of Trump's campaign aide, Carter Page, was criticized for procedural errors, as highlighted in a 2019 Inspector General report.

Key Takeaway:

While Russian interference in the 2016 election was real, accusations that Trump or his team directly colluded with Russia were not supported by the investigation's findings.

2. The Ukraine Phone Call and Impeachment

The Accusation:

Trump's July 2019 phone call with Ukrainian President Volodymyr Zelensky sparked allegations that Trump pressured Ukraine to investigate Hunter Biden, son of political rival Joe Biden, in exchange for military aid. This led to Trump's first impeachment.

The Impeachment Process and Outcome:

4. **The Inquiry:** Democrats in the House of Representatives accused Trump of abusing his power by leveraging U.S. military aid for political gain. Trump defended his actions, claiming the phone call was "perfect" and denied any quid pro quo.
5. **The Articles of Impeachment:** Trump was charged with:
    1. Abuse of Power
    2. Obstruction of Congress
6. **The Senate Trial:** Trump was impeached in the House but acquitted by the Republican-controlled Senate in February 2020. No evidence was presented that directly linked military aid to an investigation.

Key Takeaway:

While the phone call raised ethical concerns, Trump's acquittal indicated that the Senate did not find the evidence sufficient to remove him from office.

3. Tax Return Controversies and the "Paying No Taxes" Myth

The Accusation:

Trump faced accusations of avoiding taxes or paying little to no federal income taxes for year

Chapter 9: January 6: Insurrection or Political Narrative?

A Breakdown of What Really Happened on January 6

On January 6, 2021, a large crowd of Trump supporters gathered in Washington, D.C., to protest the certification of the 2020 presidential election results. While the day began with peaceful demonstrations, it escalated into a breach of the Capitol Building, sparking allegations of an "insurrection." This section explores the sequence of events, the actions of participants, and the broader implications.

- **The Timeline of Events:**
    - Trump's speech at the Ellipse emphasized peaceful protest, urging supporters to "peacefully and patriotically make [their] voices heard."
    - Shortly after the speech, segments of the crowd marched to the Capitol, where barriers were breached, and a group entered the building.
    - Law enforcement response varied, with some officers overwhelmed while others allowed entry into restricted areas.
- **Key Questions:**
    - Was the breach pre-planned, spontaneous, or incitedInvestigations uncovered a mix of factors, including pre-organized groups like the Proud Boys and Oath Keepers.
    - Were all participants insurrectionistsEvidence shows a wide spectrum of behavior, from peaceful protesters to violent actors.

The Role of Spin and Media Framing

The media played a pivotal role in shaping public perceptions of January 6. Language like "insurrection," "domestic terrorism," and "coup attempt" became widespread, creating a narrative of unprecedented rebellion.

- **Selective Coverage:** Footage of violent clashes dominated headlines, while instances of peaceful protests or calls for calm were often downplayed.
- **Double Standards:** Comparisons to prior protests in 2020 highlight inconsistencies in framing similar events.

Highlighting Evidence That Has Been Ignored or Downplayed

Several pieces of evidence and testimonies have been overlooked in the mainstream narrative:

- **Law Enforcement Failures:** Intelligence reports warned of potential violence, yet security preparations were inadequate.
- **Entrapment Concerns:** Reports and whistleblower testimonies raised questions about undercover agents and informants.
- **Selective Release of Footage:** Hours of surveillance video remain unreleased, fueling speculation about withheld evidence.

Conclusion

January 6 remains a polarizing event, with interpretations shaped by political affiliations and media framing. While violence occurred and security was breached, labeling the day as an "insurrection" overlooks critical context and evidence. This chapter encourages readers to consider the full scope of events and question the narratives presented.

Chapter 10: Donald Trump's Record: Facts vs Spin

Economic Achievements: A Booming Economy

During Donald Trump's presidency, the United States experienced significant economic growth, particularly in the early years of his administration. The economy witnessed record-breaking milestones, including **historic low unemployment rates** and **substantial stock market gains**.

- **Record Low Unemployment**: By early 2020, before the COVID-19 pandemic, the U.S. unemployment rate dropped to **3.5%**, the lowest in half a century. Unemployment rates for key demographic groups—including African Americans, Hispanics, and women—reached historic lows. Trump's emphasis on deregulation, tax cuts, and pro-business policies fostered an environment that encouraged job creation and economic growth.

- **Stock Market Gains**: The stock market flourished under Trump, with the Dow Jones Industrial Average surpassing **30,000 points** for the first time in history. Investors enjoyed strong returns, benefiting retirement portfolios and pensions.

Tax Reforms: Relief for Businesses and Individuals

Trump's administration passed the **Tax Cuts and Jobs Act of 2017 (TCJA)**, one of the most significant overhauls of the U.S. tax code in decades.

- **Corporate Tax Cuts**: The corporate tax rate was reduced from **35% to 21%**, making U.S. businesses more competitive globally. This reform incentivized companies to reinvest in the U.S. economy, contributing to job creation and domestic manufacturing growth.

- **Individual Tax Relief**: Personal tax brackets were adjusted, leading to lower taxes for many middle-class families. Standard deductions were nearly doubled, simplifying tax filings and increasing take-home pay.

Media Spin: Critics of the tax reforms argued that they primarily benefited corporations and the wealthy, dismissing the tangible benefits seen by middle-class Americans, small businesses, and the economy as a whole.

Peace Agreements: The Abraham Accords

One of Trump's most notable foreign policy achievements was the **Abraham Accords**, a series of historic peace agreements between Israel and several Arab nations, including the **United Arab Emirates (UAE), Bahrain, Sudan, and Morocco**.

- These agreements marked a breakthrough in Middle Eastern diplomacy, fostering economic, cultural, and security cooperation between former adversaries. The Abraham Accords demonstrated that peace could be achieved without conceding to longstanding demands that often stalled negotiations.

Media Spin: Mainstream media coverage often downplayed the significance of the Abraham Accords, framing them as mere economic arrangements rather than groundbreaking steps toward regional stability. Some critics argued that Trump's approach neglected the Palestinian cause, overlooking the broader context of the agreements.

America First Policies: Trade, Immigration, and Manufacturing

Trump's **America First** agenda prioritized U.S. interests in trade deals, immigration policies, and revitalizing domestic manufacturing.

- **Trade Agreements**: Trump renegotiated the **North American Free Trade Agreement (NAFTA)**, replacing it with the **U.S.-Mexico-Canada Agreement (USMCA)**. The new agreement brought significant improvements for American workers, including better labor protections and more favorable terms for the U.S. automotive industry.

- **Immigration Policies**: Trump's administration implemented stricter border control measures to combat illegal immigration and human trafficking. Initiatives included constructing sections of the border wall and adopting policies like **Remain in Mexico** to manage asylum claims.

- **Manufacturing Renaissance**: Trump's focus on tariffs and trade fairness encouraged companies to bring manufacturing back to the U.S., resulting in a resurgence in industrial employment and investment.

Media Spin: Critics often portrayed Trump's trade policies as protectionist and damaging to global alliances, ignoring the economic benefits they brought to American workers. Similarly, immigration policies were framed as harsh and inhumane without acknowledging the complexities of border security and illegal immigration.

How Successes Were Spun into Negatives

Throughout Trump's presidency, the mainstream media often shaped public perception of his policies and accomplishments through selective reporting, framing, and editorial bias.

- **Economic Growth**: While unemployment reached record lows, the media frequently credited these achievements to broader economic trends or dismissed them as the continuation of prior administrations' policies.

- **Tax Reform**: The narrative focused heavily on corporate benefits, downplaying the gains for middle-class families and small businesses.

- **Peace Agreements**: The Abraham Accords were sometimes reported as insignificant or incomplete because they did not resolve the Israeli-Palestinian conflict.

- **America First Agenda**: Trade and immigration policies were often described as isolationist or xenophobic, ignoring their focus on strengthening U.S. sovereignty and economic independence.

Conclusion

Donald Trump's presidency brought measurable achievements in the economy, foreign policy, and domestic manufacturing, but these successes were frequently overshadowed or spun negatively by mainstream media outlets. By separating **facts from spin**, it becomes evident that Trump's policies had tangible, positive impacts on American prosperity, security, and global diplomacy.

Part IV: The Future of America and the World

Chapter 11: Shattering the Imperial Order: Trump's Global Strategy to Restore Sovereignty

In a world marked by manufactured chaos, economic suppression, and perpetual war, one man has dared to challenge the entire post-World War II order: Donald J. Trump. While most observers reduce his politics to slogans or sound bites, they miss the deeper reality—Trump is engaged in a historic confrontation with a centuries-old system of imperial control rooted in globalist institutions.

This chapter explores how Trump's foreign and domestic strategies represent the most significant threat to the postwar globalist elite since the fall of the Soviet Union—and why they are doing everything in their power to stop him.

A G7 Walkout That Shook the World

In an event largely overshadowed by crisis headlines, President Trump's sudden departure from the G7 Summit in Calgary marked more than a foreign policy move—it was a declaration of independence from the globalist order. Standing next to Canadian Prime Minister Mark Carney, a symbol of postwar global economic policy, Trump publicly condemned the 2014 removal of Russia from the G8.

"You wouldn't have a war right now if you had Russia in."

These weren't just diplomatic remarks—they were a direct indictment of the G7's agenda. Trump made it clear: **their system is the problem.** The G7 doesn't represent global cooperation; it represents the machinery of managed conflict, where sovereign nations are sacrificed to preserve elite control.

A Strategy of Sovereign Partnerships, Not Perpetual War

In contrast to decades of regime change wars and intelligence-led coups, Trump's approach favors dialogue and national sovereignty. He has had multiple discussions with Vladimir Putin about Russia's role as a mediator in the Israel-Iran crisis, a move which would have been unthinkable in the Cold War mindset that still dominates Western strategy.

While the neoconservative class and mainstream media scream betrayal, Trump understands something deeper: **true peace requires treating former enemies as potential partners**—not permanent pawns in geopolitical games.

This strategic realignment isn't weakness; it's wisdom. By engaging Russia and signaling caution with China, Trump is refusing to play by the rules of a broken imperial game. He is prioritizing American interests while rejecting the idea that endless war equals global leadership.

Challenging the British Post-War Imperial System

Behind much of the opposition to Trump's agenda lies a centuries-old force—the British imperial system, now operating through modern proxies: NATO expansionists, transnational finance, legacy intelligence networks, and compliant U.S. politicians.

From Iran to Ukraine, global instability is routinely manufactured to protect this structure. The 1953 British/CIA coup in Iran, for example, replaced a democratic government with a monarchy aligned to Western interests. This manipulation of nations has become the norm under globalist policy.

Trump's goal is to **dismantle this entire framework**, not simply make minor adjustments. He envisions a world where America works with sovereign nations based on mutual benefit, not global empires.

A Domestic Revolution: The Blue-Collar Boom

While foreign policy garners headlines, Trump's economic policies are just as revolutionary. In his first five months, blue-collar wages rose nearly **2%**, the largest increase in 60 years. By focusing on manufacturing, energy independence, and immigration reform, he revived the dignity of work for millions.

Consider the ICE raid on a meatpacking plant in Omaha. The next day, **American citizens lined up to apply for jobs**—a moment symbolic of Trump's deeper belief: **American prosperity should never depend on exploitation or globalist labor loopholes.**

This renaissance challenges the neoliberal model that outsourced jobs and imported poverty to drive up corporate profits. Trump's policies prove that a nation doesn't need war and open borders to thrive—it needs leaders who put its citizens first.

Sabotage from Within: Neocons and RINOs

Despite this momentum, Trump's efforts face constant sabotage—not just from Democrats, but from **Republicans infected by globalist ideology.** Senate RINOs and neocons continue to weaken Trump's economic reforms.

They've worked to gut his "one big beautiful bill," stripping out manufacturing incentives, tax relief for tipped workers, and protections for Medicaid—all of which are cornerstones of Trump's working-class revolution.

This sabotage is no accident. It is **a defense of empire**, not America.

Toward a New Global Coalition

Trump's vision is bolder than any of his predecessors': a new alliance built around **Russia's natural resources, China's manufacturing strength, and America's innovation and capital markets.** Add India, and you have a multipolar world no longer controlled by the financial centers of London or Brussels.

This is not a betrayal of American values—it is a **return to them.** Cooperation, sovereignty, and mutual benefit once defined America's foreign outlook. Trump is restoring that legacy.

Globalists fear this because it ends their centuries-long ability to pit nations against each other. If sovereign states cooperate, the empire dies.

The Fight for the Future: Sovereignty or Subjugation

At its core, this battle isn't just about Trump—it's about choosing between two futures:

- A **world of sovereign republics**, working together to raise prosperity, dignity, and peace.
- Or a **world of managed decline**, where perpetual war, propaganda, and debt control every life.

Trump is not perfect, but he represents the clearest break from the globalist cycle of destruction in our lifetime. That's why the attacks are relentless. That's why the media distorts everything he does. Because if people understood the **depth** of this shift, they'd rise up and demand it.

Conclusion: The Realignment Has Begun

This is not a time for hesitation. Trump's global and economic strategies are not random—they are coordinated steps in a larger realignment to restore national sovereignty, dismantle imperial structures, and reignite American prosperity.

He's not just fighting for the United States—**he's showing the world how to fight back.**

If the world follows his lead, the 400-year-old imperial order collapses—and a new era begins.

Chapter 12: The Rise of Cryptocurrency: The Next Revolution

As the global financial landscape evolves, cryptocurrency has emerged as a disruptive force, revolutionizing how people view money, transactions, and financial freedom. With its decentralized structure, blockchain technology, and promise of independence from traditional financial systems, cryptocurrency offers an alternative to legacy banking systems that many believe are outdated or inefficient.

This chapter explores how Trump's views align with fostering a future-ready economy, the potential of cryptocurrency as part of this vision, and dispels myths surrounding its role in achieving financial freedom.

The Cryptocurrency Revolution

Cryptocurrency is more than a passing trend; it is a financial and technological revolution. At its core, cryptocurrencies like Bitcoin, Ethereum, and other decentralized digital assets rely on blockchain technology—a secure, transparent, and decentralized ledger that eliminates intermediaries such as banks.

The benefits of cryptocurrency are multifaceted:

- **Decentralization**: Power and control over financial transactions are shifted away from centralized authorities, giving individuals more autonomy.

- **Lower Transaction Costs**: Peer-to-peer transactions bypass banks, reducing fees and speeding up cross-border payments.

- **Financial Inclusion**: People without access to traditional banking systems can participate in the digital economy.

- **Inflation Hedge**: Cryptocurrencies like Bitcoin are often seen as digital gold, offering protection against fiat currency devaluation.

As governments and central banks grapple with economic crises and rising debt, cryptocurrencies present a decentralized alternative that protects individual financial sovereignty.

Trump's Views: A Future-Ready Economy

While Trump's relationship with cryptocurrency has been nuanced, his broader economic principles—centered on deregulation, innovation, and financial independence—align with the core philosophy of a cryptocurrency-driven economy.

- **Pro-Innovation Policies**:
  Trump has consistently supported policies that promote technological advancement and entrepreneurship. Cryptocurrencies and blockchain technology represent the frontier of financial innovation, offering opportunities for job creation, investment, and national economic growth.

- **Reducing Regulatory Overreach**:
  Excessive regulations often stifle progress. Trump's emphasis on reducing unnecessary regulatory burdens could foster an environment where cryptocurrency businesses, developers, and investors can thrive while maintaining necessary safeguards.

- **Strengthening Financial Freedom**:
  Trump's economic policies have traditionally prioritized empowering individuals to have more control over their finances. Cryptocurrency's decentralized nature aligns with this vision, allowing individuals to manage their wealth independently of traditional banking systems.

- **America's Competitive Edge**:
  Countries like China have launched centralized digital currencies, and nations worldwide are exploring blockchain applications. Under Trump's leadership, America could position itself as a global leader in cryptocurrency innovation by encouraging investment and technological development within its borders.

Dispelling Myths About Cryptocurrency and Financial

Freedom

Despite its potential, cryptocurrency is often misunderstood. Misconceptions about its security, volatility, and legitimacy have created skepticism. Dispelling these myths is essential for understanding the real value of cryptocurrency:

- **Myth 1: Cryptocurrency Is Only for Criminal Activity**
  While early headlines linked cryptocurrencies to illicit activities, blockchain's transparency makes it far more traceable than cash. Law enforcement agencies increasingly use blockchain data to track and prevent financial crimes.

- **Myth 2: Cryptocurrency Is Too Volatile to Be Taken Seriously**
  While cryptocurrencies experience price fluctuations, volatility is a feature of emerging markets. As adoption grows and regulations stabilize, cryptocurrencies are becoming more reliable. Additionally, stablecoins (digital currencies pegged to fiat currencies) offer a less volatile option for everyday transactions.

- **Myth 3: Cryptocurrency Has No Real-World Use**
  The use cases for cryptocurrencies are expanding rapidly:
  - Cross-border remittances provide affordable alternatives for international money transfers.
  - Smart contracts enable automated agreements, reducing costs and inefficiencies.
  - Blockchain applications are revolutionizing supply chains, healthcare, and governance.

- **Myth 4: Cryptocurrency Will Replace Traditional Currencies Overnight**
  Cryptocurrencies are not meant to replace fiat currencies immediately but rather complement them, offering individuals and businesses more financial options. Over

time, digital currencies could integrate into global financial systems alongside traditional money.

The Role of Cryptocurrency in Financial Freedom

At its heart, cryptocurrency embodies financial freedom:

- **Empowering the Individual**: By removing intermediaries, cryptocurrencies allow individuals to control their finances, store wealth securely, and transact without restrictions.
- **Protecting Against Government Overreach**: In countries with economic instability, cryptocurrencies offer citizens an escape from hyperinflation, bank collapses, and financial censorship.
- **Promoting Transparency and Trust**: Blockchain technology ensures every transaction is recorded, reducing fraud and increasing accountability in financial systems.

Trump's focus on self-reliance and economic empowerment aligns with these principles, making cryptocurrency a natural component of a future-ready economy.

Conclusion

The rise of cryptocurrency marks the next financial revolution—one built on decentralization, innovation, and individual empowerment. While challenges remain, Trump's policies of fostering innovation, reducing regulatory burdens, and promoting economic freedom align with the needs of a cryptocurrency-driven economy.

By embracing cryptocurrency and blockchain technology, the United States can position itself as a leader in the global financial future. For individuals, it offers not only financial opportunities but also the promise of true financial independence.

In a world where traditional systems face increasing scrutiny, cryptocurrency stands as a symbol of progress, resilience, and freedom—values that resonate with Trump's broader vision for

America.

Chapter 13: The Awakening of the Public

In an age of information overload, the public is beginning to see through the veil of gaslighting and propaganda. For years, mainstream narratives have shaped public opinion, often obscuring truths and silencing dissenting voices. Now, a global awakening is underway. People are questioning the status quo, seeking alternative sources of information, and demanding transparency.

This chapter examines how gaslighting and propaganda are being exposed, the critical role of alternative media, whistleblowers, and independent journalism, and why a well-informed citizenry is essential for a functioning democracy.

How Gaslighting and Propaganda Are Being Exposed

For decades, mass media has held unparalleled influence over public opinion, acting as both informer and gatekeeper. However, this power has been misused to manipulate perceptions through:

- **Gaslighting**: Convincing the public to doubt their own experiences or observations.
- **Selective Coverage**: Reporting only certain facts while ignoring opposing viewpoints.
- **Framing and Language**: Using emotionally charged words to steer public sentiment.

The rise of digital communication has accelerated public awareness. With unprecedented access to information, people now have the tools to verify claims, fact-check narratives, and critically analyze mainstream media messaging. Social media platforms, once controlled by algorithms favoring curated content, are now being used as battlegrounds for truth.

- **Exposing Bias**: Consumers are increasingly aware of ideological biases in legacy media outlets.
- **Breaking Through Censorship**: Efforts to silence dissenting opinions have backfired, sparking curiosity and

driving people to explore alternative perspectives.
- **Independent Fact-Checking**: Citizens themselves are becoming fact-checkers, holding institutions accountable in real time.

This shift has exposed longstanding agendas and challenged the narrative monopoly held by a few powerful voices. The public is waking up to the importance of questioning authority, demanding facts over opinions, and seeking transparency.

The Role of Alternative Media, Whistleblowers, and Independent Journalism

The decline of trust in legacy media has paved the way for alternative voices:

- **Alternative Media**: Platforms such as independent podcasts, video channels, and citizen-led news websites have gained popularity for their raw, unfiltered reporting. Unlike traditional media outlets, which are often influenced by corporate interests, alternative media prioritizes grassroots perspectives and open discourse.
- **Whistleblowers**: Courageous individuals have stepped forward to expose corruption, unethical practices, and systemic failures. From government agencies to corporate conglomerates, whistleblowers reveal the hidden truths that institutions attempt to conceal.
    - Examples like Edward Snowden (NSA surveillance) and Julian Assange (WikiLeaks) have sparked global debates on privacy, freedom, and government overreach.
    - Whistleblowers serve as a reminder that transparency often comes at great personal risk.
- **Independent Journalism**: Journalists who refuse to conform to media conglomerates are driving the awakening. These individuals embrace investigative

reporting, uncovering stories that challenge official narratives.

- Platforms like Substack and independent podcasts provide journalists with the freedom to pursue stories without editorial interference.
- Citizen journalists are increasingly filling the void, offering firsthand accounts of events and bypassing traditional media filters.

These voices play a critical role in fostering accountability and offering alternative perspectives on critical issues such as public policy, international relations, and economic reforms.

The Importance of a Well-Informed Citizenry

A functioning democracy depends on an informed public. When citizens have access to diverse, accurate, and unbiased information, they are empowered to make decisions that align with their values and interests.

- **Critical Thinking**:
  The ability to question, analyze, and interpret information is vital for dismantling propaganda. An informed citizenry challenges misinformation and seeks evidence before forming opinions.

- **Civic Engagement**:
  Awareness inspires action. When individuals understand the forces shaping their lives—economically, politically, and socially—they are more likely to participate in civic activities, from voting to advocacy.

- **Accountability**:
  A knowledgeable public holds institutions accountable. Governments, corporations, and media are forced to act transparently when citizens demand answers and refuse to accept half-truths.

- **Protection of Freedoms**:

A poorly informed population is vulnerable to manipulation, censorship, and loss of liberties. The awakening of the public ensures that free speech, free thought, and individual rights remain protected.

Conclusion

The awakening of the public marks a turning point in history. As gaslighting and propaganda are exposed, people are reclaiming their ability to think critically and question the narratives presented to them. Alternative media, whistleblowers, and independent journalists are leading this charge, offering hope for a future where truth triumphs over manipulation.

A well-informed citizenry is not just a safeguard against tyranny; it is the cornerstone of a thriving democracy. As people awaken to their role in shaping society, they become the architects of change —ensuring that power remains in the hands of the people, where it truly belongs.

The age of blind trust is ending, and a new era of accountability, truth, and public empowerment is on the horizon.

Chapter 14: The Financial Shift to ISO 20022

The global financial system is undergoing a profound transformation. For decades, the infrastructure that powers cross-border payments and financial messaging has remained relatively unchanged, relying heavily on outdated technology. However, the rise of blockchain, digital assets, and a need for faster, cheaper, and more transparent financial transactions has accelerated the push for modernization.

At the heart of this change is **ISO 20022**, a new financial messaging standard that promises to revolutionize the way money moves across the globe. March 2025 marks a critical deadline as U.S. banks and financial institutions must comply with this system. In this chapter, we'll examine what ISO 20022 is, why it matters, and how compliant cryptocurrencies like **XRP** and **XLM** are positioned to play a pivotal role in this new era of finance.

What is ISO 20022?

ISO 20022 is an international standard for electronic data interchange between financial institutions. It allows for the transmission of richer, more structured, and standardized payment data, leading to:

- **Improved Efficiency**: Faster and more accurate transactions.
- **Transparency**: Greater visibility into payment processes for both senders and recipients.
- **Cost Reduction**: Streamlined systems that lower processing costs.
- **Seamless Integration**: Enabling global financial systems to communicate effectively.

The standard replaces legacy systems like SWIFT MT messages, which have been in place for over four decades. By adopting ISO 20022, financial institutions can ensure interoperability, data transparency, and real-time payments that align with modern technological advancements.

Why It Is Revolutionizing Cross-Border Payments

Cross-border payments have traditionally been slow, expensive, and inefficient due to outdated systems, intermediaries, and currency conversions. ISO 20022 changes the landscape by:

5. **Enhancing Data Quality**: Rich, structured messages reduce errors and delays in payments.
6. **Real-Time Processing**: Faster settlements eliminate unnecessary waiting periods.
7. **Global Standardization**: A common language for financial messaging ensures consistency across borders.
8. **Facilitating Blockchain Integration**: The structured nature of ISO 20022 makes it compatible with blockchain solutions that promise speed, transparency, and efficiency.

For businesses, banks, and everyday consumers, this translates to faster payments, lower fees, and more reliable cross-border financial transactions.

Why March 2025 is a Game-Changer

The March 2025 compliance deadline for U.S. banks is a pivotal moment. At that point, ISO 20022 will become the **global standard** for financial messaging, driving massive adoption across financial institutions worldwide.

- **SWIFT Migration**: SWIFT, the current dominant global payment messaging system, is shifting to ISO 20022 to maintain relevance. Banks must upgrade their systems to remain connected to the global economy.
- **Adoption by Central Banks**: Major economies, including the European Union, the United States, and Asia-Pacific countries, are integrating ISO 20022 into their financial frameworks.
- **Implications for the U.S.**: Banks and payment systems

must overhaul their processes to meet the compliance deadline or risk losing access to the global financial network.

This shift is a once-in-a-generation opportunity to reshape the financial system, and it will require advanced technologies like blockchain and cryptocurrencies to meet its demands.

The Role of Blockchain and Crypto in ISO 20022

Blockchain technology and cryptocurrencies are uniquely suited to support the ISO 20022 standard. Unlike traditional systems, blockchain enables:

- Real-time settlement of payments.
- Decentralized networks for secure, transparent, and low-cost transactions.
- Seamless cross-border transfers without intermediaries.

Among the key cryptocurrencies positioned for ISO 20022 integration, **XRP** and **XLM** stand out:

1. XRP – The Bridge Currency

4. **What It Does**: XRP, through RippleNet, is designed to facilitate instant cross-border payments with minimal fees.

5. **ISO 20022 Compliance**: Ripple's payment network and technology align with ISO standards, making XRP a top candidate for adoption by banks and financial institutions.

6. **Bank Partnerships**: Ripple has already partnered with hundreds of banks worldwide to solve cross-border payment inefficiencies.

2. XLM – Connecting People and Systems

- **What It Does**: Stellar (XLM) focuses on low-cost peer-to-peer payments and financial inclusion, enabling fast and affordable money transfers.
- **ISO 20022 Compliance**: XLM's blockchain is ready to

integrate with financial messaging systems to support global payments.

- **Use Cases**: From remittances to business transactions, Stellar provides scalable solutions for connecting individuals and institutions.

The Ripple Effect: Why Compliant Cryptos Matter

ISO 20022 will drive demand for compliant digital assets capable of meeting the new standards for speed, efficiency, and transparency. As global adoption increases, compliant cryptocurrencies like XRP and XLM are positioned to benefit significantly:

4. **Institutional Adoption**: Banks will rely on XRP and XLM for real-time cross-border transactions.
5. **Price Surge Potential**: Increased utility and institutional demand will drive value for compliant cryptos.
6. **First-Mover Advantage**: XRP and XLM's readiness for ISO 20022 places them ahead of competitors, creating a unique investment opportunity.

Conclusion

ISO 20022 represents the financial revolution of our time. By March 2025, the shift will be complete, and the traditional payment systems will be replaced by blockchain-integrated solutions that align with this global standard. Cryptocurrencies like **XRP** and **XLM** are not just participants in this transformation—they are the enablers.

For those paying attention, this is a historic opportunity to capitalize on the shift to a more efficient, transparent, and decentralized financial system. The time to understand, prepare, and invest is **now**.

Chapter 15: XRP and XLM: The Leaders in the New Financial System

As the financial world pivots toward blockchain-based solutions and ISO 20022 compliance, two cryptocurrencies have emerged as frontrunners in this revolution: **XRP** and **XLM**. While both are built for speed, scalability, and efficiency, each serves a distinct purpose. Together, they offer the infrastructure to transform the global financial system, solving critical inefficiencies and unlocking new possibilities for individuals, businesses, and banks.

In this chapter, we will explore the roles of XRP and XLM, their unique strengths, and why they stand out as key players in the future of finance.

XRP – The Bridge Currency

XRP, created by Ripple Labs, was specifically designed to bridge the gaps in cross-border payments and liquidity issues in the global financial system. RippleNet, the network powered by XRP, enables banks, financial institutions, and payment providers to transfer money instantly, securely, and at a fraction of the cost of traditional systems.

How XRP Solves Cross-Border Payment Inefficiencies

- **Speed**: XRP transactions settle in 3-5 seconds, compared to SWIFT payments, which can take days.
- **Low Cost**: XRP fees are minimal, often less than a penny, making it cost-efficient for both high- and low-value transactions.
- **Liquidity**: XRP acts as a bridge currency, eliminating the need for pre-funded nostro/vostro accounts. This improves capital efficiency for banks and businesses.
- **Scalability**: Ripple can process 1,500 transactions per second (TPS), far exceeding the capabilities of traditional networks like SWIFT.

Adoption by Banks and Financial Institutions Worldwide

RippleNet has partnered with over **300 financial institutions** globally, including:

- Santander
- Standard Chartered
- Bank of America
- SBI Holdings

These partnerships demonstrate the real-world utility and institutional confidence in Ripple's technology. Many banks are already testing XRP to replace legacy systems and prepare for ISO 20022 compliance.

Predictions for XRP's Future Value

Given XRP's pivotal role in the new financial system, experts predict significant price appreciation as adoption accelerates:

- **Institutional Demand**: Increased use of XRP by banks will drive demand and liquidity.
- **Utility Value**: As cross-border transactions grow, XRP's role as the bridge currency will expand exponentially.
- **Regulatory Clarity**: Positive legal outcomes (e.g., Ripple's case with the SEC) will reduce uncertainty and attract further investment.

Projection: Analysts believe XRP could experience exponential growth, reaching $5–$10 in the near future and beyond as ISO 20022 adoption scales up.

XLM – Empowering Peer-to-Peer Transactions

Stellar (XLM) is designed to facilitate fast, low-cost peer-to-peer payments and financial inclusion. Unlike Ripple, which primarily targets institutions, Stellar focuses on connecting individuals, businesses, and underserved populations with affordable financial services.

Stellar's Focus on Connecting People and Systems

- **Affordable Transactions**: XLM enables near-instant payments for fractions of a cent, making it ideal for microtransactions and remittances.
- **Financial Inclusion**: Stellar's open network empowers the unbanked to participate in the global economy without relying on intermediaries.
- **Decentralized Exchange**: Stellar supports asset tokenization, enabling individuals and businesses to trade digital currencies, commodities, and even fiat-backed stablecoins.

Use Cases for Individuals, Businesses, and Banks

- **Remittances**: XLM provides a fast, low-cost solution for sending money across borders—especially valuable for migrants sending money home.
- **Small Businesses**: Businesses can accept and send payments globally without high fees or delays.
- **Central Bank Digital Currencies (CBDCs)**: Stellar is working with governments and organizations to develop blockchain-based digital currencies that integrate into the existing financial system.

Notable partnerships include:

4. **IBM World Wire**: Stellar powers IBM's cross-border payments platform.
5. **Ukrainian Government**: Stellar is collaborating to develop Ukraine's national digital currency.

Why These Coins Stand Out

Both **XRP** and **XLM** are uniquely positioned to thrive in the new financial system due to their focus on utility, efficiency, and regulatory clarity.

1. Regulatory Clarity and Adoption Trends

- **XRP**: Ripple is achieving regulatory clarity through legal battles, positioning XRP as a compliant asset for institutional adoption.
- **XLM**: Stellar has prioritized partnerships with governments and organizations to align with evolving regulations and global standards.

2. Comparison to Bitcoin and Ethereum

While Bitcoin and Ethereum paved the way for cryptocurrencies, they fall short as tools for a scalable, efficient financial system:

- **Transaction Speed**:
    - Bitcoin: ~10 minutes
    - Ethereum: ~15 seconds
    - XRP/XLM: ~3–5 seconds
- **Transaction Fees**:
    - Bitcoin: High and volatile
    - Ethereum: Gas fees fluctuate with network congestion
    - XRP/XLM: Less than a penny, regardless of transaction size.
- **Energy Consumption**: XRP and XLM use environmentally friendly consensus mechanisms, unlike Bitcoin's energy-intensive Proof of Work.

Conclusion

As the financial world transitions to ISO 20022, XRP and XLM are emerging as leaders in this new era of finance. RippleNet's XRP is solving cross-border payment inefficiencies for banks and institutions, while Stellar's XLM is empowering peer-to-peer transactions and financial inclusion.

These compliant, utility-driven cryptocurrencies stand apart from speculative assets like Bitcoin and Ethereum. Their adoption by major financial institutions, governments, and businesses positions them as the foundational assets of the future global financial system.

For readers, this is not just an opportunity to witness history—it's an invitation to participate. Understanding and investing in XRP and XLM today could mean being on the ground floor of a revolution that will reshape how money moves across the world.

Chapter 16: The Opportunity of a Lifetime

The world stands on the brink of a financial revolution driven by blockchain technology and ISO 20022-compliant cryptocurrencies. Just as Bitcoin and Ethereum transformed how we think about digital assets, a new wave of cryptos like **XRP** and **XLM** is poised to reshape the financial system—this time with institutional backing and real-world utility.

Understanding market cycles, acting early, and recognizing the significance of ISO 20022 adoption can create life-changing opportunities for investors who are prepared. This chapter will explore why early adoption matters, what financial experts predict for 2024–2025, and practical steps to start investing safely and securely.

Understanding Market Cycles in Crypto

The cryptocurrency market has historically moved in cycles, often driven by adoption milestones, investor sentiment, and macroeconomic events.

Lessons from Bitcoin and Ethereum

- **Bitcoin**: In 2010, Bitcoin was worth fractions of a cent. By 2021, it reached **$69,000** per coin. Early adopters saw **unparalleled returns** because they understood its long-term potential.

- **Ethereum**: Launched in 2015 at $0.30, Ethereum grew to over **$4,800** by 2021. Its utility and adoption drove exponential growth.

The common denominatorEarly adoption. Those who recognized the potential of these digital assets before mainstream acceptance reaped significant rewards.

Why ISO 20022 Changes Everything

Unlike speculative cryptos of the past, ISO 20022-compliant assets like **XRP**, **XLM**, and similar coins are uniquely positioned:

- **Real-World Use Cases**: These assets solve real financial problems, such as cross-border payments, liquidity management, and financial inclusion.
- **Institutional Adoption**: Banks, payment providers, and governments are preparing to integrate these cryptos into the global financial system.
- **Regulatory Alignment**: Compliance with ISO 20022 sets these assets apart from non-compliant alternatives, ensuring they are ready for institutional use.

The March 2025 compliance deadline will accelerate institutional adoption, pushing these assets into mainstream use and driving significant price appreciation.

Predicted Growth for 2024–2025

Financial experts predict **exponential growth** for ISO 20022-compliant cryptocurrencies as adoption increases:

- **XRP**
    - Ripple's partnerships with over 300 financial institutions will drive demand for XRP.
    - As banks replace SWIFT systems with RippleNet, XRP's role as a bridge currency will solidify.
    - **Expert Projection**: XRP could reach $10–$20 or higher as global adoption scales up.
- **XLM**
    - Stellar's focus on peer-to-peer payments, remittances, and CBDCs positions it as a cornerstone for financial inclusion.
    - Growing partnerships (e.g., IBM and governments) will expand XLM's utility globally.
    - **Expert Projection**: XLM could see price growth to $2–$5, driven by institutional and retail use.

- **Other ISO 20022-Compliant Assets**
    - **IOTA (MIOTA)**: A leader in IoT (Internet of Things) transactions.
    - **Quant (QNT)**: Focused on blockchain interoperability for enterprise adoption.
    - **Hedera (HBAR)**: Offering fast, secure, and energy-efficient transactions.
    - These coins are expected to see significant upward movement as they align with the new financial system.

How Blockchain Adoption by Banks Will Drive Prices Higher

Banks and financial institutions moving toward blockchain technology will bring unprecedented liquidity into the crypto market. The ISO 20022 mandate will act as a catalyst, forcing institutions to adopt these assets to remain competitive. As demand surges and supply remains fixed, prices are expected to rise exponentially.

Timing the Market: Why "Getting in on the Ground Floor" Matters

The greatest opportunities arise before mass adoption. In the early stages of any revolutionary technology—whether it's the internet, smartphones, or cryptocurrency—those who act first see the most significant gains.

Why Now Is Critical

3. The **March 2025 ISO 20022 compliance deadline** will drive institutional adoption of XRP, XLM, and other compliant assets.
4. Banks and governments are already positioning themselves, but mainstream investors are largely unaware of this shift.
5. As awareness grows, prices will begin to reflect the

massive demand and utility of these digital assets.

The Window of Opportunity

- **Pre-Adoption Stage**: We are currently in the pre-adoption phase, where prices remain undervalued.
- **Mass Adoption Phase**: As institutions fully integrate ISO 20022, prices will increase significantly.
- **Post-Adoption Stage**: Prices will stabilize at higher levels, but the life-changing growth potential will have passed.

The time to act is **now**—before the market catches up.

Practical Steps to Start Investing Safely and Securely

To capitalize on this opportunity, follow these steps to invest in ISO 20022-compliant cryptocurrencies safely:

3. **Educate Yourself**
    1. Research XRP, XLM, and other compliant assets.
    2. Understand their utility, partnerships, and future potential.
4. **Choose a Secure Exchange**
    1. Use trusted exchanges like Coinbase, Binance, or Kraken to purchase XRP and XLM.
5. **Set Up a Secure Wallet**
    1. Use hardware wallets (e.g., Ledger Nano) or trusted software wallets to store your crypto securely.
6. **Start Small and Diversify**
    1. Begin with a modest investment and increase gradually.
    2. Diversify your holdings among XRP, XLM, and other ISO-compliant assets (e.g., IOTA, QNT,

HBAR).

7. **Avoid Scams**
   1. Be cautious of unrealistic promises and unverified platforms.
   2. Always double-check wallet addresses and exchanges before transactions.

8. **Stay Updated**
   1. Follow news about ISO 20022 adoption, Ripple, Stellar, and other blockchain projects.
   2. Use reliable sources like CoinMarketCap, CoinGecko, and independent analysts.

Conclusion

The shift to ISO 20022 is not just another trend—it's a **once-in-a-lifetime financial transformation** that will reshape how money moves across the globe. Cryptocurrencies like **XRP** and **XLM** are at the forefront of this revolution, offering early investors a unique opportunity to position themselves ahead of the mainstream curve.

History has shown that those who act early—before the masses wake up—reap the greatest rewards. The time to educate yourself, take action, and secure your stake in the future of finance is **right now**.

This is the ground floor. Don't miss it.

Chapter 17: Dispelling Myths About Cryptocurrency

Cryptocurrency, despite its growing adoption and technological breakthroughs, is still surrounded by skepticism and misinformation. Myths about risk, volatility, and mainstream adoption often deter individuals from exploring its vast potential. However, not all cryptocurrencies are created equal, and those with real-world utility—such as **ISO 20022-compliant assets like XRP and XLM**—are paving the way for a more efficient and transparent financial system.

In this chapter, we will dispel the most common myths surrounding cryptocurrency and explain why now is the time to pay attention.

"Crypto is Too Risky or Volatile"

Volatility has been a defining characteristic of cryptocurrencies, particularly in the early years of Bitcoin and Ethereum. While market fluctuations are still present, it's important to understand that **ISO 20022-compliant cryptocurrencies** are fundamentally different:

- **Backed by Real-World Utility**
    - Unlike speculative assets, XRP and XLM have clear use cases: solving inefficiencies in global payments and financial systems.
    - RippleNet (XRP) and Stellar (XLM) are already being used by major banks, payment providers, and governments to enable fast, low-cost, and cross-border transactions.
- **Institutional Adoption Reduces Risk**
    - Institutions are integrating ISO 20022-compliant assets into their systems, which adds legitimacy and stability to these digital assets.
    - As banks and businesses rely on XRP and XLM for

operations, these assets will move from speculative investments to integral components of global finance.

- **Mature Market Conditions**
    - Regulatory clarity for assets like XRP is reducing uncertainty, while market infrastructure (exchanges, wallets, and custodial services) is more secure and robust than ever before.

Key Point: Volatility is natural in an emerging market, but ISO 20022-compliant cryptos are built on **utility** and **institutional adoption**, making them more stable and promising for long-term growth.

"Banks Won't Use Crypto"

A common misconception is that banks are resistant to cryptocurrency. However, Ripple (XRP) and Stellar (XLM) have already established themselves as solutions to the very problems banks face: inefficiencies, high fees, and slow cross-border payments.

Proof of Adoption by Major Banks and Institutions

- **RippleNet's Partnerships (XRP):**
    - Ripple has partnered with **over 300 financial institutions** worldwide, including:
        - **Santander**
        - **Bank of America**
        - **Standard Chartered**
        - **SBI Holdings**
    - These partnerships highlight Ripple's role as a bridge between traditional banking systems and blockchain technology.

- **Stellar's Collaborations (XLM):**
    - Stellar's network focuses on financial inclusion and peer-to-peer transactions. Key partnerships include:
        - **IBM World Wire**: A global payment network using Stellar for cross-border settlements.
        - **Ukrainian Government**: Developing a national digital currency on Stellar's blockchain.
        - **Financial Service Providers**: Numerous payment firms and remittance companies use Stellar for fast, low-cost transactions.
- **ISO 20022 Adoption Mandate**
    - By **March 2025**, banks and financial institutions will need to comply with ISO 20022. XRP and XLM, already ISO 20022-compliant, offer the most practical blockchain-based solutions for integrating this new messaging standard.

Key Point: Major banks and financial institutions are not just adopting crypto—they are actively partnering with Ripple and Stellar to revolutionize global payments.

"I Missed the Crypto Boat"

Another myth is that the greatest opportunities in cryptocurrency have already passed. People often cite Bitcoin and Ethereum as examples of "missed" opportunities. However, the current landscape presents **a new window of opportunity**—one driven by utility, institutional adoption, and ISO 20022 compliance.

Why You Haven't Missed Out

- **The Early Adoption Phase for ISO 20022**

- While Bitcoin and Ethereum were speculative early investments, XRP and XLM are just beginning their role as foundational assets in the global financial system.
- The **March 2025 deadline** for ISO 20022 compliance means banks and financial institutions are preparing to adopt these assets right now.

- **Institutional Liquidity Has Yet to Enter**
  - Once ISO 20022 is fully implemented, trillions of dollars in institutional capital will flow into compliant digital assets.
  - XRP and XLM are positioned to benefit directly, driving demand and price appreciation.

- **Historical Patterns**
  - Like Bitcoin in 2010 and Ethereum in 2015, XRP and XLM are currently undervalued relative to their future potential.
  - As the financial world shifts to blockchain-based systems, these assets will experience exponential growth.

A Second Chance for Generational Wealth
- Many who dismissed Bitcoin or Ethereum in their early stages regretted not acting. XRP, XLM, and other ISO 20022-compliant coins represent a **second chance** to get in on the ground floor of a financial transformation.

Conclusion

The myths surrounding cryptocurrency—whether about volatility, institutional rejection, or missed opportunities—are rooted in misinformation and misunderstanding. XRP and XLM are not speculative "get-rich-quick" assets; they are tools designed to solve real-world problems and facilitate a more efficient global financial system.

- **They are already being adopted by banks, businesses, and governments.**
- **They are compliant with ISO 20022, the new global standard for financial messaging.**
- **Their true value is yet to be fully realized as we approach the March 2025 deadline.**

The opportunity to position yourself for life-changing gains still exists. By understanding the role of XRP, XLM, and other compliant assets, you are equipping yourself to capitalize on the **next financial revolution**.

The boat hasn't sailed—it's just about to leave the dock. Now is the time to get on board.

Chapter 18: How to Get Started in Cryptocurrency Safely

As the global financial system transitions to ISO 20022 and compliant cryptocurrencies like **XRP** and **XLM** gain momentum, there has never been a better time to begin investing. However, entering the cryptocurrency space can feel intimidating, especially with concerns about security, scams, and market volatility.

This chapter provides a practical, step-by-step guide to help you invest in XRP, XLM, and other ISO 20022-compliant coins safely, while balancing risk and reward to maximize your potential returns.

Step-by-Step Guide to Investing

Getting started with cryptocurrency requires following a few essential steps to ensure your investments are secure and accessible.

1. Opening a Secure Crypto Wallet

A crypto wallet is a digital tool that allows you to securely store and manage your cryptocurrencies. There are two primary types:

- **Hot Wallets** (online): Accessible via the internet, suitable for beginners and active trading.
    - Examples: Trust Wallet, Exodus, MetaMask.
- **Cold Wallets** (offline): Hardware wallets offer maximum security for long-term holding.
    - Examples: Ledger Nano X, Trezor Model T.

Steps to Open a Wallet:

- Download a trusted wallet app or purchase a hardware wallet from the official site.
- Follow the setup instructions to create a wallet and back up your **private keys** or **recovery phrase** (usually 12–24 words).
- Store your recovery phrase securely—**never share it with**

anyone.

2. Choosing Reliable Exchanges to Purchase XRP, XLM, and Compliant Coins

A cryptocurrency exchange allows you to buy, sell, and trade digital assets. To ensure safety, choose well-established platforms with a history of security and regulatory compliance.

Recommended Exchanges:

4. **Coinbase**: User-friendly and regulated in the U.S.
5. **Binance**: Global platform offering a wide variety of cryptos, including XRP and XLM.
6. **Kraken**: A trusted exchange with a strong security record.
7. **Bitstamp**: Popular for purchasing XRP, with a long-standing reputation.

Steps to Buy Cryptocurrency:

4. Create an account on a reputable exchange and complete the required identity verification (KYC).
5. Deposit funds using a bank transfer, debit/credit card, or approved payment method.
6. Search for **XRP, XLM**, or other ISO 20022-compliant coins and make your purchase.
7. Transfer your purchased crypto to your secure wallet for long-term storage.

Diversifying Your Portfolio

While XRP and XLM are leaders in the ISO 20022 space, there are other compliant assets worth considering. Diversification reduces risk and increases the potential for balanced growth.

Other ISO 20022-Compliant Cryptocurrencies

- **IOTA (MIOTA)**: Designed for the Internet of Things (IoT), IOTA facilitates feeless and scalable microtransactions.

- **Algorand (ALGO)**: Known for its speed, scalability, and sustainability, ALGO powers decentralized finance and enterprise solutions.
- **Hedera Hashgraph (HBAR)**: Focused on high-speed, secure, and energy-efficient transactions, HBAR is backed by enterprises like IBM and Google.
- **Quant (QNT)**: A leader in blockchain interoperability, enabling seamless integration between multiple blockchains and traditional financial systems.

Balancing Risk and Reward

A well-rounded portfolio combines high-potential cryptos like XRP and XLM with other promising projects:

- **Low Risk**: XRP and XLM (institutional backing and real-world use cases).
- **Medium Risk**: ALGO, HBAR, IOTA (expanding adoption and utility).
- **Higher Risk**: Emerging ISO-compliant coins with less mainstream traction.

Example Portfolio Allocation:

- 50% XRP/XLM (core assets)
- 20% ALGO, HBAR
- 20% IOTA, QNT
- 10% cash reserve (for market opportunities).

Avoiding Scams

Cryptocurrency's rapid growth has attracted scammers eager to exploit uninformed investors. Recognizing legitimate opportunities versus hype is critical to protecting your investments.

Common Types of Scams

- **Phishing Attacks**: Fake websites or emails tricking users into sharing wallet recovery phrases or private keys.
    - **Prevention**: Always verify the URL and use two-factor authentication (2FA) on exchanges.
- **Pump-and-Dump Schemes**: Scammers artificially inflate a coin's price and sell at the peak, leaving unsuspecting investors with losses.
    - **Prevention**: Avoid unknown, low-market-cap coins promoted on social media.
- **Fake Wallets and Apps**: Fraudulent wallets steal your crypto.
    - **Prevention**: Use official websites to download wallets or apps.
- **Guaranteed Returns**: Any promise of guaranteed profits is a red flag.
    - **Prevention**: Invest in cryptos with real-world use cases and do your research.

Key Steps to Safeguard Your Investments

- **Do Your Research**: Always investigate a project's purpose, partnerships, and real-world adoption.
- **Verify Sources**: Use trusted platforms (CoinMarketCap, CoinGecko) for information.
- **Store Securely**: Transfer assets to a hardware wallet for long-term security.
- **Avoid "Get-Rich-Quick" Claims**: Focus on projects like XRP and XLM with proven value.

Conclusion

Entering the cryptocurrency space doesn't have to be complicated or risky. By following a step-by-step approach—selecting secure wallets, choosing reliable exchanges, and diversifying wisely—you can position yourself for success in the ISO 20022-driven financial revolution.

XRP, XLM, and other compliant assets offer not just an investment opportunity but the chance to participate in reshaping the global financial system. By investing safely and avoiding scams, you can capitalize on this unique moment in history and build a foundation for long-term financial freedom.

The opportunity is here—the tools are in your hands. **Take action, stay informed, and invest wisely.**

Chapter 19: The Future of Finance Is Now

The financial world is undergoing its most profound transformation in history. For decades, centralized systems, slow payments, and high fees have left individuals, businesses, and even governments frustrated. Today, blockchain technology, ISO 20022, and cryptocurrencies like **XRP** and **XLM** are ushering in a new era of financial transparency, efficiency, and accessibility.

This chapter explores what these changes mean for everyday people, how banks and businesses are adopting blockchain, and why now is the time to take action. The future of finance isn't coming—it's already here.

What This Means for Everyday People

For too long, financial systems have favored the few while burdening the many. Blockchain-based solutions, driven by ISO 20022-compliant assets, are breaking down barriers and creating opportunities for everyone:

- **Increased Financial Access**
    - Millions of unbanked individuals globally will gain access to financial services through blockchain-powered networks like Stellar (XLM).
    - People in remote or underserved regions can send and receive payments instantly, without reliance on traditional banks or intermediaries.
- **Lower Fees and Faster Payments**
    - Cross-border payments that once took **3-5 days** will now settle in **seconds** with assets like XRP.
    - Transaction fees will drop dramatically. For instance:
        - Traditional wire transfers cost $20–$50.
        - XRP and XLM transactions cost fractions

of a cent.
- Everyday expenses like sending money abroad, paying for services, or buying goods will become faster and more affordable.

- **Empowerment Through Financial Ownership**
    - With cryptocurrencies, individuals control their wealth without dependence on banks.
    - Blockchain enables greater transparency—people will see where their money goes, preventing hidden fees or manipulation.

Real-World Impact Example:

Imagine a migrant worker sending money home to their family. Instead of waiting days and losing significant amounts to fees, they can send money instantly via Stellar (XLM) at near-zero cost. This improves lives, ensures more money stays in families, and empowers individuals globally.

How Banks and Businesses Are Adopting Blockchain

Banks and businesses are at the forefront of this revolution. Rather than resisting change, many institutions are embracing blockchain and cryptocurrencies to remain competitive, efficient, and compliant with new standards like ISO 20022.

1. Financial Institutions

- Major banks are adopting RippleNet and XRP to facilitate instant, cross-border payments.
- Stellar (XLM) is collaborating with governments and fintech companies to create Central Bank Digital Currencies (CBDCs), making money transfers seamless.
- Blockchain integration reduces operational costs, increases speed, and improves transparency for both banks and customers.

Examples of Adoption:

- **Ripple's Partnerships**: Over 300 banks and financial institutions, including Santander, SBI Holdings, and Bank of America.
- **IBM's World Wire**: Powered by Stellar, it enables instant cross-border payments for businesses and governments.
- **CBDC Initiatives**: Stellar's blockchain is being used to develop national digital currencies, ensuring seamless integration with the global financial system.

2. Businesses

4. Companies are using blockchain for supply chain transparency, smart contracts, and digital payments.
5. Small businesses benefit from lower transaction costs, enabling them to expand their reach globally without prohibitive fees.

Key Benefits:

4. Real-time financial settlements.
5. Enhanced data security and accuracy.
6. Lower operating costs and reduced reliance on intermediaries.

The adoption of blockchain isn't just theoretical—it's happening **now**, and businesses that adapt early will thrive in the coming financial landscape.

Final Call to Action

The future of finance is no longer a distant vision—it is unfolding before us. The shift to ISO 20022, combined with blockchain technology and compliant cryptocurrencies like **XRP** and **XLM**, represents the greatest financial revolution of our time.

Wake Up to the Revolution Before It's Too Late

- **The March 2025 Deadline**: Banks and financial institutions are preparing to integrate ISO 20022-compliant systems. This shift will create unprecedented demand for XRP, XLM, and other compliant assets.
- **Opportunity for Everyday People**: You don't need to be a financial expert or institutional investor to benefit. Understanding this shift and taking action now will place you ahead of the curve.
- **Generational Wealth**: Early adopters of Bitcoin and Ethereum changed their lives. XRP, XLM, and ISO-compliant assets are offering the next great opportunity.

How Understanding and Participating in This Shift Will Change Lives

For those who pay attention, this is not just an investment opportunity—it's a chance to:

4. Break free from outdated, costly financial systems.
5. Build financial independence and freedom.
6. Contribute to a fairer, more inclusive financial future.

By recognizing the utility and adoption of XRP, XLM, and other ISO 20022-compliant coins, you are participating in a movement that will reshape global finance. Those who act now will be the ones who reap the greatest rewards when the rest of the world finally wakes up.

Conclusion

The future of finance is here, and you have the chance to be part of it. Blockchain technology and ISO 20022-compliant assets like XRP and XLM are not just buzzwords—they are the building blocks of a new, efficient, and inclusive financial system.

The tools are in your hands. The opportunity is before you. Don't wait until it's too late to understand, invest, and capitalize on the **financial revolution of a lifetime**.

This is your moment. **Act now, and change your future forever.**

Part V: Restoring the Republic

Reclaiming Sovereignty, Borders, and the American Identity

This part captures Trump's deeper mission—not just economic renewal or media takedown, but the **reestablishment of America as a sovereign constitutional Republic.** It brings together border policy, law and order, patriotism, and the symbolism of the flag.

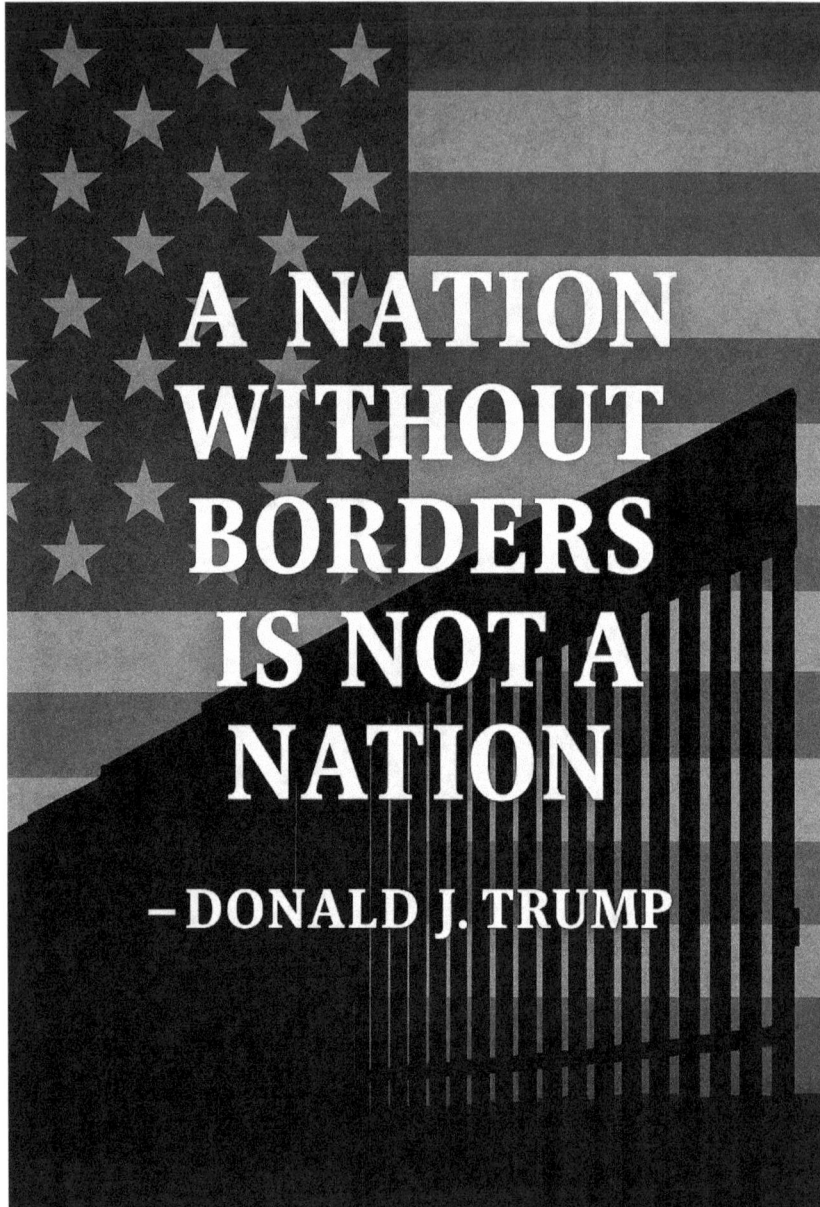

Chapter 20: Securing Our Borders, Defending Our People

"A nation without borders is not a nation." – Donald J. Trump

From the very beginning of his 2016 campaign, Donald Trump made one thing unequivocally clear: **America must reclaim control of its borders to remain a sovereign nation.** The mainstream media mocked the promise to build a wall. Political elites called it xenophobic. But the American people knew better. They understood that border security isn't about hatred or fear—it's about **law, order, protection, and identity**.

Trump's call to deport **criminal illegal aliens** wasn't a partisan dog whistle—it was a **constitutional necessity**. No country can survive if it cannot decide **who enters, who stays, and under what terms.**

❖ Trump's Early Vow: Law and Order at the Border

During his presidency, Trump prioritized the removal of **criminal non-citizens**, including gang members, traffickers, and repeat offenders. He empowered ICE and Border Patrol with the tools they needed, restored morale in law enforcement, and began constructing **hundreds of miles of border wall** along the southern frontier.

This wasn't just symbolic—it had real results:

5. Illegal border crossings dropped dramatically during peak enforcement periods.
6. ICE deported thousands of criminals with prior convictions who had re-entered the country.
7. Cartel movement was disrupted in high-traffic corridors.

For Trump, protecting the American people was not optional—it was sacred. **Every illegal entry, every crime committed by someone who never had the right to be here, represented a failure of the system to defend its citizens.**

❖ The Biden Border Breakdown: Chaos by Design

When Joe Biden took office, the border policies shifted almost overnight—from enforcement to appeasement. Executive orders dismantled key Trump-era initiatives, halted wall construction, and severely limited ICE's ability to carry out deportations.

The result?

- Record-breaking **illegal crossings**, exceeding **2 million per year**
- Massive influxes of **fentanyl, human trafficking, and cartel activity**
- Border agents overwhelmed and demoralized
- Cities and states declaring emergencies due to the burden of illegal immigration

While the media tries to frame the issue as a humanitarian concern, the truth is chilling: the Biden administration's open-border policies have placed Americans in danger, destabilized communities, and empowered criminal networks.

❖ Holdman and the Rise of Local Resistance

As the federal government fails to uphold its constitutional duty, **states and local leaders have stepped up**, inspired by Trump's original America First stance. Leaders like **Holdman** (and governors such as Abbott and DeSantis) are proving that **the will of the people is not dead**—it's simply going local.

5. State-led deportation programs targeting criminals
6. National Guard deployed to protect state borders
7. Legal pushback against federal overreach on immigration policy

These actions reflect the awakening Trump sparked—a belief that **states and citizens have a right and a responsibility to defend their land, their families, and their future.**

❖ Why Borders Are the First Line of Sovereignty

Borders are more than fences and checkpoints—they're the **physical manifestation of a nation's will to exist.**

When borders collapse:

- Crime crosses without resistance.
- Labor markets are destabilized.
- Cultural cohesion erodes.
- Citizenship becomes meaningless.

But when borders are protected:

- Law regains authority.
- Nations flourish under self-determination.
- The people feel safe and sovereign.

Trump understood that without strong borders, the American Republic itself was at risk. The Constitution loses meaning when foreign nationals can enter at will. Elections become compromised. Taxpayer systems are abused. **A borderless America is a post-American empire—and that's exactly what globalists want.**

❖ Conclusion: The Wall Was Just the Beginning

The fight for the border is the fight for the **soul of the nation**.

Donald Trump didn't just propose physical walls—he challenged a spiritual wall of denial, apathy, and surrender that had consumed D.C. for decades. Today, with everyday citizens, governors, and officials like Holdman carrying that torch, the movement to **restore American sovereignty** is alive and expanding.

But this isn't a battle that ends at the Rio Grande.

It's a fight for **identity, safety, and legacy**. And it belongs to all of us.

Without borders, there is no nation. Without security, there is no freedom. Without sovereignty, there is no America.

Chapter 21: Sovereignty or Submission — The Crossroads We Face

"We will no longer surrender this country or its people to the false song of globalism." – Donald J. Trump

Every generation faces a defining choice—a moment where it must decide whether to **preserve the values that built a nation**, or submit to the forces working to erase them.

Today, America stands at such a crossroads.

The battle is no longer left vs. right. It's not Democrat vs. Republican. It's **sovereignty vs. submission**. It's the Republic vs. the Empire. And Donald J. Trump, by challenging both parties, the media, and the globalist elite, exposed the **true fault line** running through modern history: **Will America remain a free, sovereign nation—or become just another client state in a managed global system?**

❖ What Is Sovereignty—And Why Does It Matter?

Sovereignty is the power of a nation to control its borders, laws, economy, and culture without outside interference.

It is **the cornerstone of the Constitution**.
It is **the basis of the Declaration of Independence**.
It is **what generations of Americans have fought and died to defend**.

Without sovereignty, we lose:

- The power to decide **who becomes a citizen**
- The authority to determine **our own trade, energy, and foreign policy**
- The ability to protect our culture, economy, and values from being overwritten by global dictates

Trump understood this. That's why he **withdrew from the TPP, renegotiated NAFTA into the USMCA, stood up to NATO overreach**, and **demanded fairness in trade and diplomacy**.

These weren't "unilateral" moves—they were **sovereign moves**.

- ❖ How Globalists Undermine Sovereignty

The modern globalist agenda operates through **subtle erosion, not direct invasion.**

- **Trade deals** that prioritize multinational profits over local jobs
- **Open border policies** that flood communities with illegal migration, destabilizing wages and public services
- **Endless foreign wars** that deplete national will, treasure, and unity
- **Digital surveillance and financial systems** that weaken personal and national independence

Globalists claim their vision brings unity, peace, and progress—but what they **really bring is dependency**, debt, censorship, and control.

Trump was the first president in a generation to push back. That's why they tried to destroy him.

- ❖ Restoring National Will: Trump's Sovereignty Doctrine

Trump's policies were not random—they followed a **clear doctrine of national will**:

- **Energy independence** through domestic oil, gas, and innovation
- **Immigration control** through walls, deportations, and merit-based entry
- **Economic re-industrialization** through tariffs and tax reform
- **Foreign policy restraint** through peace negotiations, not regime change

These weren't isolationist. They were **foundational**.

Trump wasn't withdrawing from the world—he was **reasserting America's right to engage on its own terms.**

❖ The 2024 Crossroads: Trump's Return or America's Fall?

As we head into the next election, the stakes have never been higher.

It's not just about personalities—it's about **philosophies of governance**.

Trump's America	Globalist America
Sovereign Nation	**Borderless Entity**
Free Citizens	**Managed Populations**
Strong Military, No Endless Wars	**Weaponized Foreign Policy**
Economic Self-Reliance	**Dependency on Foreign Labor and Imports**
Free Speech & Law	**Speech Codes & Legal Chaos**

Trump represents resistance to submission—and a rallying point for all who still believe America belongs to its people.

❖ Conclusion: Choose the Republic

This moment is about more than politics. It's a **civilizational decision**.

Will we live under rule by elected leaders—or global technocrats and unelected NGOs?

Will we define our future—or have it dictated by corporate think tanks and foreign banks?

Will we protect the flame of liberty—or let it flicker out under the weight of silence?

Trump has drawn the line. The choice is ours.

Sovereignty isn't just a right—it's a responsibility. We must not only vote for it. We must defend it, live it, and pass it on.

Chapter 22: The Power of the Flag — Symbol of a Reclaimed Nation

"When you open your heart to patriotism, there is no room for prejudice." – Donald J. Trump

It's more than a piece of fabric.
It's more than stars and stripes.
The American flag represents the **soul of a nation**—its struggles, its triumphs, and its enduring belief in freedom. When Donald Trump raised two massive flagpoles outside the White House to fly **giant American flags**, he wasn't just planting banners in the ground—**he was sending a message to the world: The Republic stands. And it will not fall.**

In an age of collapsing borders, globalist manipulation, and cultural confusion, **symbols matter more than ever**. The flag reminds us **who we are**, **what we defend**, and **where we must go next**.

❖ The Flag as a Political Statement

Throughout history, tyrants have torn down the flags of the free, and revolutionaries have raised new banners of hope.

When Trump hoisted those flags—against the backdrop of a White House under siege by media, bureaucrats, and ideological enemies—it was a **strategic act of defiance**. He was reclaiming territory not just physically, but spiritually.

The media called it "showmanship."
Critics called it "nationalism."
But for millions of Americans, it was **a rallying cry**.

This is your house. This is your country. And this is your moment to stand.

❖ What the Flag Represents

The American flag carries more than color—it carries meaning. Each thread woven into it stands for:

- **Liberty**, bought with blood
- **Sovereignty**, guarded by law
- **Justice**, rooted in moral clarity
- **Unity**, forged through trials and victory
- **Sacrifice**, made by generations of patriots

It flies over every military base, every embassy, and every school—not as a relic of the past, but as a **reminder of what must be defended.**

When we salute it, we are not honoring a government—we are honoring **a promise**.

❖ The Attack on Symbols and Patriotism

The globalist machine knows the power of symbols. That's why it relentlessly works to **shame**, **erase**, or **redefine** American identity.

- Flag-burning is called "free expression," while flag-waving is labeled "extremism."
- Standing for the national anthem is mocked, while kneeling is celebrated.
- Patriotic speech is suppressed under the guise of "misinformation."

WhyBecause **they know that the flag unites**—and unity is the enemy of division-based control.

Trump's unapologetic patriotism reversed that trend. He brought **flags back to rallies, back to schools, back to the streets**. And in doing so, he reminded Americans that **national pride is not hate—it's heritage**.

❖ The Symbolism of Trump's Twin Flags at the White House

Trump's decision to install **twin flagpoles**—one American flag, one presidential—was deeply symbolic.

- **Two pillars**: One for the people, one for the Constitution
- **Soaring high**: A visible sign to every visitor, ally, or adversary that **America is led by someone who stands for her**
- **Unignorable**: Positioned where the press had to see them daily, they became a **silent but thunderous reminder** of the America First mission

These weren't ceremonial flags. They were **battle standards**—marking a presidency rooted in revival.

❖ Conclusion: Let the Flag Fly Again

If the wall is the **shield**, the flag is the **banner**.

It reminds us what we fight for—not just against tyranny, but **for liberty**. Not just against invasion, but **for sovereignty**. Not just against lies, but **for truth**.

The more they try to hide the flag…
The higher we must raise it.
The more they try to shame it…
The prouder we must carry it.
The more they try to silence it…
The louder we must speak what it stands for.

The flag belongs to no party. It belongs to the Republic. And to reclaim that Republic, we must raise it higher than ever before.

CHAPTER 23

THE REPUBLIC RESTORED

THE AWAKENING IS NOW

Chapter 23: The Republic Restored — The Awakening Is Now

"We are transferring power from Washington, D.C., and giving it back to you, the people." – Donald J. Trump, Inaugural Address, 2017

The moment is no longer coming.
The moment is now.

America is not just facing a political realignment. We are experiencing a **spiritual, cultural, and civilizational awakening**. From the border crisis to global currency shifts, from the suppression of truth to the resurgence of patriotic pride, one thing has become clear:

The American Republic is under attack—but it is not defeated.

Thanks to the leadership of Donald Trump—and the millions of awakened citizens rising in his shadow—**we now stand on the edge of restoration.**

This chapter is the final call. The final charge. The final line.

❖ A Republic—If We Can Keep It

Benjamin Franklin once warned that America had been given "a republic—if you can keep it."
Those words have never been more prophetic.

We were never promised ease.
We were never guaranteed safety.
What we were given was **a system designed to work only if** *we the people* **engaged.**

Trump has done his part:

- He exposed the media.
- He challenged the deep state.
- He redefined patriotism.
- He reignited the fire of self-governance.

But **he cannot save the Republic alone.**

- ❖ This Is Your Awakening

What began as a political campaign became a movement. What became a movement is now a **national rebirth**. The Trump Effect isn't just about one man—it's about the **millions who have woken up to the truth.**

- Truth about who controls our money.
- Truth about how we're manipulated by fear.
- Truth about what our Constitution really means.
- Truth about why we must now stand—not later, not someday, but **now.**

- ❖ Restoration Requires Participation

Restoring the Republic doesn't happen in Washington—it begins at home.

You restore the Republic when you:

- **Speak truth**, even when it's unpopular
- **Support leaders** who put America first
- **Protect your family**, community, and local values
- **Educate others** about the lies, the history, and the hope
- **Prepare financially** for the transition from fiat to blockchain-powered freedom
- **Refuse to comply** with systems designed to enslave, shame, or erase you

- ❖ This Is the Final Battle—And the Beginning

We are not returning to the past—we are **resurrecting the promise of the Republic**.

Trump's role in this era will be studied for generations. But you—**the awakened citizen**—will determine how this story ends.

Will America fall to digital dictatorship, borderless bureaucracy, and engineered chaos?
Or will we rise with clarity, courage, and commitment?

The future is not written.
But the pen is in your hand now.

- ❖ Conclusion: The Awakening Is Now

The wall has been built. The flags have been raised. The truth has been told. Now it's time to act.

Let the globalists tremble.
Let the elites panic.
Let the corrupt scream.

Let the Republic rise.

Chapter 24: A Veteran's Vow — This Republic Shall Prevail

"Greater love hath no man than this, that a man lay down his life for his friends." – John 15:13 (KJV)
"Blessed is the nation whose God is the Lord." – Psalm 33:12

I met a man today.
He was 93 years old.
He served in Korea.
A quiet man with proud eyes and a firm grip, he told me stories of cold battles and lifelong friends now gone.

Around 15 years ago, I met another man.
He had just turned 101.
The last living survivor from his ship in World War II.
He joined the U.S. Navy when he was just **14 years old**.

And in those moments, standing by these two American giants, I realized something:

This flag we wave, this land we walk, this Republic we fight for—it was all built on their backs.

They are not just veterans.
They are **guardians of the Republic.**

❖ The Flag Is Their Blood, Stitched by Sacrifice

To some, the flag is fabric.
To others, it's controversy.
But to a veteran—it is sacred.

Every red stripe speaks of **blood shed**.
Every white stripe reminds us of the **purity of their cause**.
And every star is a soul that believed this nation was **worth dying for**.

The men and women who served didn't fight for fame or fortune.
They fought for an idea. A promise. A land.
The Promised Land.

❖ America Is the Promised Land

The God of Israel, the God of Moses, of Abraham, Isaac, and Jacob—He is a God of **freedom**, of **covenants**, and of **purpose**.

The Bible speaks of a Promised Land, a land flowing with milk and honey, a land set apart to become a light to the nations.
I believe **America is a modern extension of that promise**—a land where people of all races, faiths, and backgrounds can live free under God's law and man's Constitution.

"Every place that the sole of your foot shall tread upon, that have I given unto you." – Joshua 1:3

This is a land where liberty is not given by kings or parliaments but endowed by the **Creator Himself**.
And every force that rises to destroy this land—whether foreign or domestic—**will fail.**

❖ A Message from the Veterans

"I served. I bled. I buried my brothers. But I never lost faith."

We Veterans speak not as politicians or pundits, but as those who **offered our lives** for the flag, the Constitution, and the people of this Republic.

To the tyrants of the world:
You will not break us.

To those who despise freedom:
Your efforts are in vain.

To those who want to erase America's foundations:
We will rebuild them stronger.

This is our vow:

- The Republic will endure.

- The flag will fly.
- And the truth will outlast every lie.

❖ A Final Warning and Declaration

To all nations watching…
To every foreign entity, ideological cult, or political system that seeks to undermine America's foundations…
You will not prevail.

No religion that seeks to enslave.
No ideology that seeks to divide.
No system that replaces freedom with fear—**will ever overthrow what this Republic stands for.**

"If God be for us, who can be against us?" – Romans 8:31

This nation stands under God.
And united we stand.

❖ United We Stand: The Final Word

While the Bible doesn't have the exact phrase **"United We Stand"**, the truth behind those words is deeply biblical:

"Now I beseech you, brethren… that ye be perfectly joined together in the same mind and in the same judgment." – 1 Corinthians 1:10
"Behold, how good and how pleasant it is for brethren to dwell together in unity!" – Psalm 133:1

Unity under God is America's secret weapon.

We are not perfect—but we are principled.
We are not always united in policy—but we are united in **purpose**.
And that purpose is liberty—for all.

Let this message be heard in every nation:
The United States of America will never surrender her Republic.
Not to tyrants. Not to globalists. Not to evil.

We are awake.
We are unbreakable.
We are America.

And **this Republic shall prevail.**

✅ Conclusion: Restoring Truth, Trust, and Opportunity

In an era where information is abundant yet truth remains obscured, a rare kind of courage is required—the courage to **see clearly**, **think critically**, and **act boldly**. The storm of gaslighting, institutional manipulation, and financial confusion has led to something unexpected: **an awakening.**

Not just to misinformation.
Not just to the failing financial systems.
But to something much deeper:
A rebirth of the **American spirit**.

Across these pages, you've explored how propaganda clouds perception, how false narratives distort history, and how blockchain technology is dismantling the old financial order. You've read how Donald Trump challenged not only the media but the global system itself—and how his movement has inspired millions to **reclaim what has been stolen.**

But now, that responsibility falls to **you**.

❖ A Dual Awakening: Financial and Foundational

This is more than a call to action—it is an invitation to **take your place in history**.

Chapters 14–19 revealed the **new financial infrastructure** already forming beneath our feet:

- ISO 20022 is reshaping global payments.
- XRP and XLM are redefining what trusted money looks like.
- Institutional adoption is paving the way for global transparency and speed.
- Everyday people—not just the elite—can now take part in building **generational wealth.**

But the greatest revolution isn't in code—it's in **conviction**.

- ❖ A Nation Reawakened

In *Part V,* you saw that the battle for financial sovereignty mirrors something even more critical: the battle for **national sovereignty**.

- To restore our **borders** is to restore our identity.
- To raise the **flag** is to remember the blood that bought this freedom.
- To honor **Veterans** is to remember that **this Republic was built on sacrifice**, and **it will not fall**.

This isn't just about money.
It's about meaning.

- ❖ Seek Truth, and Then Act

  - **Think critically**: Don't accept what legacy media or broken systems say without question.
  - **Demand results**: Leadership—political or financial—must produce *real outcomes* that lift people up.
  - **Take action**: The tools are in your hands—blockchain, decentralized finance, truth-telling media, and your voice.

"Blessed is the nation whose God is the Lord." – Psalm 33:12

- ❖ Leadership Through Results

The essence of leadership is **not rhetoric—it's reality**. Whether transforming economies, defending freedom, or restoring national pride, leadership must be measured by **truth and tangible progress**.

Trump's impact, like the awakening itself, is measured not in headlines but in what millions are doing now: questioning, building, preparing, and standing tall.

- ❖ A Stronger, Resilient Republic

This is your moment.

- To awaken to truth

- To protect your family and freedom
- To participate in the financial revolution
- To restore the Republic—one heart, one household, one nation at a time

Let the world hear the message loud and clear:

This Republic will prevail.

The flag will fly.
The truth will rise.
And freedom—guided by faith, secured through action—will light the path forward.

"If God be for us, who can be against us?" – Romans 8:31

Appendices

Appendix A: Key Speeches by Donald Trump

This section includes pivotal speeches that highlight Trump's vision, policies, and stance on major issues during his leadership. Each speech reflects his emphasis on restoring economic prosperity, strengthening national security, and redefining America's role globally.

- **Inaugural Address (January 20, 2017)**
    - Key Themes: "America First," returning power to the people, and revitalizing American industry.

- **Address to the United Nations General Assembly (September 25, 2018)**
    - Key Themes: Sovereignty, fair trade, and holding nations accountable for their actions.

- **State of the Union (February 4, 2020)**
    - Key Themes: Economic achievements, workforce growth, energy independence, and foreign policy successes.

- **Speech at the World Economic Forum (January 21, 2020)**
    - Key Themes: Promoting American innovation, cutting regulations, and ensuring U.S. competitiveness in a globalized economy.

- **Announcement of 2024 Presidential Run (November 15, 2022)**
    - Key Themes: Addressing the crises facing America, restoring law and order, and building a future-ready economy.

Each speech is summarized for its key points, with excerpts included for readers to analyze Trump's message and policies directly.

Appendix B: Fact-Checked Myths and Lies Spread Over the Last Four Years

This section addresses and dispels widely circulated misinformation and false claims about Trump, his policies, and his leadership. Each myth is paired with verified facts to provide clarity and accuracy.

Myth	Fact
"Trump banned immigration from all Muslim countries."	Trump's 2017 travel ban applied to specific countries with security concerns, not all Muslim-majority nations.
"Trump never condemned white supremacy."	Trump explicitly condemned white supremacy on multiple occasions, including in press conferences and speeches.
"Trump's tax cuts only benefited the wealthy."	The Tax Cuts and Jobs Act reduced taxes for the middle class and increased take-home pay for working families.
"Trump mishandled the COVID-19 response."	Trump initiated Operation Warp Speed, resulting in vaccines being developed in record time.
"Trump ignored climate issues."	Trump prioritized energy independence but supported clean energy technologies alongside fossil fuel development.

Each entry includes supporting evidence, data, or direct statements for readers to independently verify the facts.

Appendix C: Resources and Further Reading for Independent Research

This section provides a comprehensive list of resources to help readers conduct their own research, analyze diverse perspectives, and draw informed conclusions.

Books

4. *"The Case for Trump"* by Victor Davis Hanson
5. *"Trump and the American Future"* by Newt Gingrich
6. *"Great Again: How to Fix Our Crippled America"* by Donald J. Trump
7. *"Unmasking the Administrative State"* by John Marini

Independent Media Sources

- **The Epoch Times**
- **Just The News** (John Solomon)
- **The Daily Wire**
- **X.com (formerly Twitter)** for real-time updates and diverse commentary

Speeches and Statements

- Official transcripts of Trump's speeches available at the **National Archives**
- Press briefings and interviews: **C-SPAN, WhiteHouse.gov Archive**

Alternative Journalism and Investigative Platforms

- **Project Veritas** – Investigative journalism uncovering media and institutional misconduct.
- **Substack** – Independent journalists offering in-depth analysis and reporting.

Documentaries and Videos

- *"The Trump Card"* directed by Dinesh D'Souza
- *"Death of a Nation"* (historical context for modern politics)
- *YouTube Channels* – Independent journalists and commentators like Tim Pool and Glenn Greenwald.

Research Databases

Conservative Fact-Checking Organizations

When discussing conservative fact-checking organizations, it is essential to recognize that the landscape of fact-checking is diverse and includes various organizations that may align with conservative values or perspectives. Here are some notable conservative-oriented fact-checking organizations:

1. The Daily Signal Fact Check

The Daily Signal, a news outlet affiliated with the Heritage Foundation, provides a fact-checking section that focuses on claims made by politicians and public figures, particularly those related to conservative policies and issues. Their approach often emphasizes accountability for statements made by liberal politicians and media.

2. Truth in Media

Founded by journalist Ben Swann, Truth in Media aims to provide an alternative perspective on news stories that are often covered from a liberal viewpoint. While not exclusively a fact-checking organization, it seeks to verify claims and provide context for various issues, especially those relevant to conservative audiences.

3. PolitiFact's "Truth-O-Meter" Ratings

While PolitiFact is generally considered non-partisan, its ratings can sometimes reflect a more critical stance towards claims made by conservative figures compared to their liberal counterparts. However, it is worth noting that PolitiFact operates under strict guidelines for transparency and methodology, which can appeal to those seeking reliable information regardless of political affiliation.

4. The Western Journal Fact Check

The Western Journal offers a fact-checking service that evaluates claims primarily related to politics and social issues from a conservative perspective. They focus on debunking misinformation they perceive as coming from left-leaning sources while promoting narratives aligned with conservative values.

5. The Federalist Fact Check

The Federalist features articles that often include fact-checks or critiques of mainstream media narratives from a conservative viewpoint. Their analysis typically challenges what they view as biased reporting or misinformation regarding conservative policies or figures.

These organizations contribute to the broader conversation about truthfulness in media but do so through lenses that may prioritize or resonate more with conservative audiences.

In summary, while there are several organizations dedicated to fact-checking within the conservative framework, their methodologies and focuses can vary significantly. Some aim for rigorous adherence to factual accuracy while others may prioritize defending specific ideological positions.

Conclusion of Appendices

These appendices are designed to give readers direct access to primary sources, fact-checking tools, and alternative viewpoints. By consulting these resources, readers can engage in critical analysis and form independent, well-informed opinions about the issues discussed throughout the book.

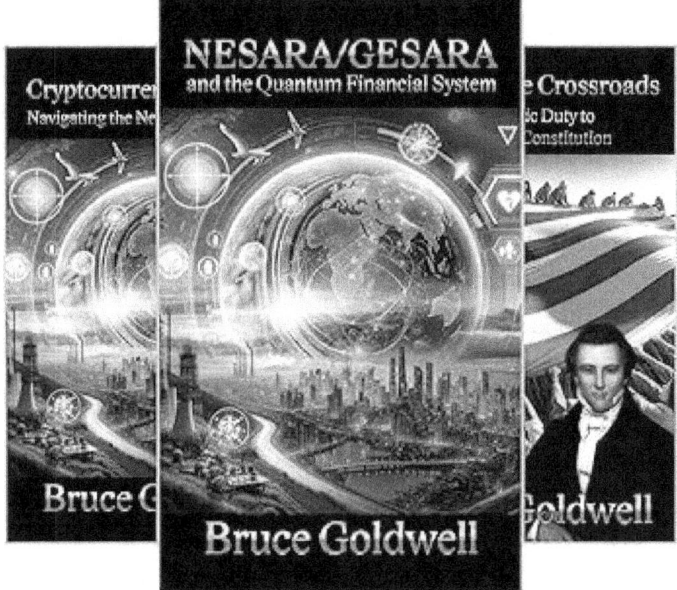

Embark on a transformative journey through the "Foundations of Freedom" series, where finance, innovation, and patriotism converge to shape the future of our nation and the world. From exploring the dynamic landscape of cryptocurrencies and decentralized finance to delving into the profound implications of constitutional duty and national security, this series offers a comprehensive exploration of the forces shaping our economic and political landscape.

Join us as we navigate the complexities of modern finance, uncovering the potential of groundbreaking innovations such as blockchain technology, the Quantum Financial System (QFS), and the NESARA/GESARA initiatives to revolutionize the way we interact with money, invest in assets, and conduct transactions. But beyond the realm of finance, the "Foundations of Freedom" series delves into broader topics that define the fabric of our society, including the enduring principles of liberty, the responsibilities of citizenship, and the quest for a more just and equitable world.

At its core, this series is a testament to the enduring spirit of American patriotism and the unwavering commitment to defending the freedoms enshrined in the Constitution. Through meticulous research, insightful analysis, and a dedication to truth and integrity, the "Foundations of Freedom" series equips readers with the knowledge and understanding they need to navigate the challenges and opportunities of the 21st century.

Whether you're a seasoned investor, a curious newcomer, or simply a concerned citizen, "Foundations of Freedom" invites you to join us on a journey of discovery, empowerment, and action. Together, let us build a future grounded in the principles of freedom, innovation, and patriotism, ensuring that the foundations of our democracy remain strong for generations to come. https://amzn.to/3Aed006

About the Author

Bruce Goldwell is an accomplished author with a diverse portfolio of over 100 books, spanning topics from personal development and the law of attraction to fantasy fiction and financial insights. His journey into writing began with the *Dragon Keepers* series, published initially by Saga Books, which quickly resonated with readers for its inspiring themes and valuable life lessons. Bruce's commitment to creating uplifting content stems from his own life experiences, including a period of homelessness during which he found mentorship from luminaries like Bob Proctor, Jack Canfield, and Mark Victor Hansen. Today, Bruce uses his platform to empower others, including aspiring authors, sharing insights and resources he's gathered over the years. As he delves into subjects like cryptocurrency, ISO 20022, and the future of finance, Bruce remains dedicated to providing accessible, thought-provoking information that inspires both seasoned readers and newcomers alike.

Www.mykindlebooks.net